Wrestling the Light

Ache and Awe
in the Human-Divine
Struggle

Prayers and Stories

BY TED LODER

WITH DRAWINGS BY ED KERNS

San Diego, California

LuraMedia ™

Other books by Ted Loder:
Guerrillas of Grace (1984)
Tracks in the Straw (1985)
No One But Us (1986)
Eavesdropping on the Echoes (1987)

© Copyright 1991 LuraMedia
San Diego, California
International Copyright Secured
Publisher's Catalog Number LM-624
Printed and bound in the United States of America

Front cover art by Ed Kerns, Easton, Pennsylvania
Front cover design by Linda Lockowitz, San Diego, California

LuraMedia
7060 Miramar Road, Suite 104
San Diego, CA 92121

Library of Congress Cataloging-in-Publication Data

Loder, Ted, date.
    Wrestling the light : ache and awe in the human-divine struggle / by Ted Loder : drawings
by Ed Kerns.
        p.   cm.
    ISBN 0-931055-79-2
    1. Prayers.   2. Christian life—Methodist authors.   I. Title.
BV245.L573   1991
242—dc20   91-37123
                                                                 CIP

CONTENTS
Prayers and Stories

FOCUSING
A Preface

Grace is probably the most central and crucial word in the vocabulary of the Christian faith. Yet, even to say quite simply that grace refers to the way, or ways, God restores us estranged creatures to Him/Herself opens the gates to deep and, I believe, irresolvable mysteries.

From the biblical witness on, our Judeo-Christian history is the history of trying to understand not only the "why" and "what" of grace, but especially the "how" of it. As grace is a gift, the expression of God's initiative toward us, the why and what of it have to do with God's freedom to be God with and for us as He/She chooses. That domain is one we glimpse, at best, only "in a mirror dimly."

But the how of grace is the intersection of the ache and awe in the human-divine struggle. The how has to do with the ways grace might come to us, shape us, restore us. The how, then, involves our discernment and experience of life's meaning, our response to this proclaimed gift. That discernment and response is the essence of the religious life, the life of the spirit, the life of faith personally, relationally, and corporately.

Though no less mysterious than the why and what of grace, the how of it becomes more immediate and urgent for us. Theologians have written innumerable volumes about the how of grace, making distinctions between such modes as actual grace, prevenient grace, sufficient grace, efficacious grace. Such distinctions can be useful and clarifying if they help us to discern the fingerprints of grace on our lives.

But this analytic process also has the effect of diminishing the dynamic quality of life, reducing the mystery to definitive categories and, worst of all in my view, making religion or faith just another area of life, and a much too narrow and specific one at that. The how of grace slips into being the "how to" of grace, and thus the particular domain of institutional religion.

Consequently, we tend to miss the more inclusive, subtle, sneaky, supposedly non-religious ways grace could be, and I trust is, operating in our lives. And we usually don't consider our responses to those non-traditional experiences of grace — or "coincidence" or meaning — as having any religious or spiritual significance, if in fact we actually take time to reflect on our responses much at all. As a result we continue in our sense of estrangement, on which I think we do reflect if only in the middle of sleepless nights or on occasions when, for some reason, we cannot escape into busyness.

So it doesn't occur to us that God's grace is always operating to restore us to Her/ Himself if we haven't had any commonly defined "religious" type experience. Therefore, our estrangement, or deprivation, includes a kind of prayerless, worshipless, joyless, one-dimensional life in which there is little trust and much anxiety.

Consistently, I come back to the telling of stories as the most congruent way to touch on at least some of the many levels of our ordinary lives in which grace works, perhaps primarily in simply sustaining us in life and giving us choices day by day, choices that convey possibilities for us to do and be something at least somewhat new and different; to move bit by incremental bit toward that freedom, peace, wholeness that salvation implies and these narratives explore.

So *Wrestling the Light* is a book of stories and prayers in which I try to express something of the way I discern grace operating in common, unreligious but, to me, quite amazing and wondrous ways to restore people to God, even though the characters in the stories might not put it that way themselves. If these characters would describe what happens as being restored, or partially restored, to themselves and to others, then surely they have begun to experience the mystery of grace, and of God, beyond tidy labels. If the experiences portrayed in this book help us discern some suggestive and significant possibilities of the mysterious how of grace in our own lives, it will be enough.

Each of these stories, in quite different form, was originally shared with my congregation in the "sermon" portion of a worship service and were, and are, reflections on particular experiences as well as products of my imagination — imagination being, I contend, a critical aspect, a dancing partner of faith. It is my hope that the stories reflect glimmers of the light with which they wrestle — light being something of a metaphor for grace in this book, and wrestling in all its sweaty, twisting, grunting, sensuous, lively, sometimes painful, often humorous and underlying fun-glad-joyful qualities being, for me, a response of faith.

The prayers in *Wrestling the Light* are intensely personal, and they appear here for the first time. These are a new form of prayer for me, something of a departure from the style usually associated with praying. Yet, I think they are rooted in the tradition of the psalms in that they are reflecting before God as a person might reflect on his/her life experience in the presence of a trusted friend. In a sense, they might be called narrative prayers. The intent is to explore and deepen a relationship with God within the stuff of life experience. As in a story, the struggle is to find meaning coming out of experience in the act of praying rather than being injected into it as a result of the prayer. That distinction may be slight and subtle, but it seems accurate and helpful to me.

In the same sense, the stories in *Wrestling the Light* are prayers in some profound way, even though the language and style are very different from those usually used in praying. But to wrestle with, and for, the light, for some meaning in life, is always a way of being in the presence of God, whether consciously or not. And to me, being in the presence of God, rather than the degree to which a person may be consciousness of God at any given moment, is what defines the heart of prayer. Of course, the more intense a person's consciousness, the deeper the experience probably will be, as witness *The Revelation To John* in the Bible and the writings of the mystical saints. Yet consciousness alone does not determine the availability of an experience of God's presence, any more than eyesight, whether keen or not, determines the existence of whatever is seen. Grace is always a gift.

In another sense, the prayers in *Wrestling the Light* are attempts to be poetic because I think poetry, in its respect for and use of words and images, is a powerful, often stunningly revealing way to express our human experiences and longings. Poets who do not intend their work to be prayers, and would rightly disavow that they are, still can have their poems read as prayers because they are honest, provocative, and they disclose profound truths in ways that move my soul. Those poems open me to God's presence in undeniable ways.

So to write prayers in a way that intends something of poetry is to try to echo that experience in a reverse but intentional way. Even as the psalms cannot be read only as poetry, however poetic they are, I share these writings not primarily as poetry but as prayers, as ways of wrestling to find meaning, to discern grace operating in life, as a means of participating with God in some small way in creating some bit of new order out of my chaos, in pointing to some shreds of light in the darkness.

A very fresh experience sums up the point of this Preface. Two weeks ago I visited a young, not traditionally religious, close friend who was dying. I sat on one side of his hospital bed and a woman friend of his stood on the other side of the bed. We talked quietly. But every so often my friend would ask, "Who is here?" The woman and I would say our names, and my friend would reply, "I know that. I mean, at the foot of the bed, down there. Who is that?" The woman and I both would assure my friend that it was no one, that she and I were the only ones in the room with him. My friend was not persuaded and kept asking. We kept telling him it was no one. The next day my friend died. Were we right in telling my friend there was no one at the foot of the bed? On the face of it, and by any measurable, verifiable standard, we were. He was medicated. He was undergoing profound neural, chemical changes in his body. He was experiencing great emotional turbulence. Any of that might reasonably explain his vision of an unknown someone at the foot of his bed.

And yet, reason can be just another form of idolatry. I think now we sadly, arrogantly over-stepped our place and power in telling my friend there was no one there. He sensed a presence. Could it not have been an angel, his guardian angel, the angel of death, of grace, there with him? Could it not have been God going about the mysterious, gracious work of restoring my friend — and the two of us on either side of the bed — to Him/Herself, overcoming what estranges us, separates us from God and from each other? The answer, the trusting answer, is "Yes, it could," though it be only a whisper, or awed silence, then a story, or poem, or prayer. The answer of faith is, "Yes, for that is surely how the grace of God comes, as strange glimmers of light into the dark, deep, holy, yet common places of our fearful, hopeful, very daily wrestling."

I am grateful for those who have wrestled this book into being with me, most of whom must remain anonymous, except these: Adam Geiger, to whom it is dedicated; Lura Jane Geiger, whose faith sustains many and me; Marcia Broucek, whose skill and support as an editor and friend have been invaluable; Ed Kerns, whose vision and talent as an artist and whose kinship in life constantly opens new dimensions to me; my staff colleagues and the people of the First United Methodist Church of Germantown, who share the journey; Mark, David, Karen, Thomas, who are wondrous light to me and whose wrestling with me is a great, saving gift; Christopher, Jonathan, Jeffrey, Nadya, who not only help me to see but to see miracles; and Jan, who is grace upon grace to me.

Theodore W. Loder
Philadelphia, Pennsylvania
September, 1991

Tumbled in your shimmering wake

At that snap of grace,
    finger of mystery against finger of purpose,
        when first you struck the light,
            scattering fire as far as forever,
O Hurler of these shining spheres,
    did you know
        that across these whirling eons
            light would set us against our own darkness?
    Did you know
        that this insistent pelting
            would break our hearts with longing,
        that its nurturing, patient power
            would pull our souls, like sap
                through sea of time,
                through root of cell,
                through fin and claw
                and thumb and tongue,
            'til life woke wondering self-aware
                and stammered out its prayers to you,
                    as now I do?
    Surely you knew
        that light would set my dreams climbing like vines
            up the shafts of chance, surprise, and promise;
        would draw my eyes to distant suns and pilgrims near,
        and lump my throat at beauty I can scarcely bear!

You are its source;
    of course, you knew
        that light is what life's wrapped around,
            what wraps itself in life,
                so truth alone can stand its glare,
        and love is its appeal,
            while justice done displays its hues
                and servants, its intent, like Christ,
                  and the lilies of the field.

O God,
>   whose cloak is light,
>>   I'm tumbled in your shimmering wake,
>>>   its scarcely weight breaks my heart again,
>>   and I cry and laugh after balance,
>>>   gasping to catch my longing, and my breath,
>>>   imagining enough to sense the unquenchable in me,
>>>   trusting enough to claim you put it there,
>>>>   beachhead of eternal light against the darkness.

So, wrestled, pinned, branded, set free,
>   I rise to pray my story, tell my prayer,
>>   a thousand, thousand tiny sparks
>>>   and I am one,
>>>>   a bit of burning dust
>>>>>   of gratitude exacting,
>>>>>>   of light turning to praise.

For Adam,
a beautiful man
whose sensitivity, courage, and love
have made music of his life, for our lives

RELATIONSHIPS

A night light against the darkness

O God,
I am tentative before you,
    confused in my clutter of misplaced dreams,
        abandoned hopes,
            tattered faith;
    shriveled by the cramp of busy-ness,
        the leak of disappointment,
            the grind of cynicism.
From this mock of shadows, this nightmare of botch,
    I turn to you,
        this prayer a night light
            against the darkness.
There is strange assurance in the turning,
    as if at the approaching of a long-lost friend.
In my brokenness glimmers an awareness
    that only what is broken,
        like bread, and hearts, can be shared;
    that love is hard, tougher than nails,
        humbling as mystery, true to life.
O Broken God,
    I would endure this love,
        swear and weep to welcome it.
So come, Lord, into my brokenness.
    Resurrect the cluttered pieces of me
        into a stronger, somewhat whole
    and make me brave
        to dream anew,
            to hope the kingdom in,
                to share the bit of truth I am
                    toward some sweeter, saving end,
        to love us creature fools hard,
            yet with a merciful, knowing heart.
Grace, then, to fear not the shadows,
    but to heed the ripples of light forever breaking in,
        bidding me rise and follow
            toward brothers, sisters,
                the promised day,
                and you.

I do not know myself yet

Holy One, I would pray
    not because you do not know me already,
        but because I do not know myself yet,
            and seek myself with you.
Shed the light of your grace upon me
    and go with me into the dark, untended,
        shameful, scary corners of my life.
Ease the frantic, swollen pride
    by which I claim too much for my efforts,
        credit too little those of others,
            and stifle gratitude to them, and you.
Soften my callous belittlement of others
    by words that blame,
        or collusions that exclude,
            and so demean and divide us all.
Straighten me out of the crippling illusion
    that my burdens are heavier
    than those of others.
Liberate me to share my struggles honestly
    so I may embrace the miracle of my humanity
    and drink, in exultation,
        the wine of others' gifts.
Visit with me my nightmare fears
    to dredge them up to light, O God;
        and help me give the furies names,
            to tame their wild, hypnotic power,
                and start to heal my waiting soul
                    and those I wounded at the furies' prod.
Undamn the juices of my passion,
    unbury the riches of my talent,
        that in the flow and wield of them,
            in my daring and my doing,
                a light will break
    and I will see my life is far more than it seems,
    and trust enough to learn by heart
        the truth of me you know so well,
            and to give by choice
                the gift it is you ask of me.

Unbutton my proud bluffs

O God of ferocious tenderness and disarming insistence,
    unbutton my proud bluffs,
        put your ear to my heart,
            listen to what I long for,
                and touch me with healing and with hope.

For I've been seduced to exhaustion
    by the siren hype of others' demands,
        but I responded to them in kind.
I've been impaled on spiky sulks
    when their needs weren't met,
        but I responded to them in kind.
I've been shriveled to bitterness
    by their blame for things gone sour,
        but I responded to them in kind.
I've been scorned to isolation
    when their arrogance forged bias into creed,
        but I responded to them in kind.
In rage and resentment I have closed down hard
    on others, and on myself —
        hearing not, forgiving not, risking not,
          turning no other cheek,
            walking no second mile,
              loving no enemy.

The darkness of doubt is upon me,
    doubt of my worth,
        my power,
          my possibilities,
            my connection with others,
              my kinship with you.

O God, separate once more the light from the darkness.

Make light of me,
    dispelling my gloomy grudges and guilty fears,
        transforming my dreary self-preoccupations
            into flicker of giggles, filament of trust,
                a kind of radiant confidence in more-than-me you.

Make light in me,
    reviving my pulseless impulse
        to mount one small revolution of trust,
            and so to lift a little light,
                span some gap,
                    pick some deadlock,
                        tip some scale toward justice.

Make light through me,
    igniting a dawn of reunion and peace,
        a dazzle of laughter,
            a glow of peace,
                a splendor of joy,
                    a great, spangly resurrection of love.

Scorched aware

O God,
I look,
    and find you looking back
        in the eyes of lover, child,
            enemy, friend, stranger,
        in the image in the mirror.
I can scarcely hold watch or long bear
        that light in eyes,
            that peering of the soul,
        your secret hidden in us like a glowing coal —
            a haunting, frightening, fascinating
                brand of Eden,
                    burning bush,
                        empty-tomb holiness.

I look,
    and am scorched aware of
        how fragile
            and how precious
                is everything I love,
                    everything I am, have, do, give.

I look,
    and you look back,
    and in the lurch and tumble of your fire,
        I glimpse again
            your power to work miracles
                by turning the few loaves and fishes
                    of my gifts, and me,
                    into food for some other lonely ones;
            your power to ignite to flame
                my look, my stretch toward you
                    and so to inspire to life
                    other wide-eyed seekers such as I.

In the light of such miracles, O God,
    let there be community,
        the welding of love and courage
            in me, and as far as I can see.

Grant me nerve to dare the wonder,
    willingness to hold watch,
        to walk in the light —
            that fierce, tender, terrible beauty,
                of your looking, your beckoning —
    that ever being burned to death,
        and life,
            by your gaze,
I may be saved, and sent again, and spent
    in the sacred seek
        toward those I can never be with wholly,
            nor yet be whole without.

The kettle of the day

O God
     never quite grasped,
        yet always at the tip
            of my tongue, my mind, my heart,
    while it's still dark
        I hear the dawn —
            winged chatter,
            feathered singing,
            black, grumpy caws,
            clatter of the early train —
    and yawning up, I put on
            the kettle of the day.

Pink and blue slowly spreads, heaven to earth,
    ineffable, inseparable, mysterious as male/female,
        timeless probe into my quick time,
            transcendence in disguise,
                disturbing, welcome reminder
                    of what I never quite remember,
                      or ever quite forget,
                          this wonder at the tip of me.

I stammer my praise, my "O-God-I'm-glad,"
    for those I love and who love me,
        though who knows the why,
            except mercy and grace,
                and the willingness to do love's long labors
                    toward love's deep rewards;
    for the sheer delight of this sexual self,
        in the sharing with a beloved sexual other;
    for laughter, music, family rough and tumbling
        to truly find each other,
            and mercifully find our way home;
    for rain on the roof,
        wine and apples,
            sentinel trees;

for hard lessons learned,
    dreams blistered into beginnings,
        and the terrible, lonely freedom of deciding;
for honest, artful words
    that unwind my too tight, tidy mind
        and entwine it to my heart;
for mistakes corrected, weaknesses owned,
     changes made, failures become teachers;
for those who show me the narrow, saving difference
    between cleverness and integrity,
        success and joy;
for the traces of wisdom
    the years have left in me;
for old friends, good stories,
    nothing to do, sitting still,
        listening, watching, thinking, praying, sleeping;
for work to go back to,
    for the sweat for bread;
for peace,
    and for justice,
        which is love with its sleeves rolled up;
for this stubbornly fertile,
    painfully abused,
        incredibly beautiful, beloved mother earth;
for this fumbling, frangible human world,
    still bathed in light,
        cradled in heaven;
and this for Christ's sake longing at the tip of me,
    and at my core,
        for what only you could make me long for.

I remember but this meager much
    and offer you my thankful prayer.

So magnificent . . . so flawed

O God, I am torn.
      Do I rant or praise?
This world is so magnificent,
      so flawed,
and I cannot divert
      my gaze,
          or heart,
              from either.
So I rage,
      shudder out my fear,
          cry my compassion
              at birth defects;
              at kids therapied bald-headed
                  playing out their short days,
                      while parents watch, helplessly;
              at twisted limbs,
                  spastic bodies,
                     blind eyes,
                         vacant minds;
              at AIDS,
                  like war, thinning a generation,
                     stealing too much talent away,
                       mocking youth and us,
                         malevolent as a drought;
              at so many plagues, so many blights,
                  such endless, frenzied feeding,
                  germ on cell,
                     glitch on gene,
                        species on species;
           and at this ugly coil of violence
              lurking in my shadows,
                  striking to wreak its havoc.
I despair.

Damnit God,
       why these terrible, hellish,
             insidious, all-too-perfect imperfections?
     Has it gotten out of hand?
     Has it fallen too far?
     Have I?
I really cannot bear it!
     Can you?
Is this what the cross is about?
     I half-trust it is, and yet . . .
          I rage and lift the whole to you.
Which means I praise, as well,
     for beauty past all telling of it,
          which no one in the least deserves;
     for the urge of love that stirred the earth
          and folded in the dust of us,
              and raised us up and set us free,
                 yet pounds within our veins;
     for all that summons from my heart,
          for the songs it strangely knows,
              for those heights my words don't reach,
                 but hurl them up, I do —
                    like courage, truth, and ecstasy,
                    and the hardest one, trust.
Yes, both rage and praise,
     the bag is mixed in me as in the world,
          and to deny one is to cancel the other.
So, as an act of trust,
     and trustworthiness,
          I take these steps,
              first limp, then leap,
                 toward lonely, loving you
         and learn to live
             as best I can,
                with all there is
                   in this wondrous, puzzling world,
               and with myself, as well,
                 and, gracefully, with you.

The bullies who follow me home

O artful Weaver of the oft-violated,
    yet finally inviolable web of human ties,
        these common, sticky, holy connections
            that define each, and link all,
I bring my friends home with me to you
    only to find the bullies, leeches, ciphers,
        follow me as well,
    those I would leave behind but cannot
        because they are so much a part of me,
            and I of them, at last.
So here they are, I cannot keep them out:
    the fools I laugh at,
        and treat less well than I would
            if I weren't so easily embarrassed;
    the obnoxiously sure who grind at me,
        but perhaps could not
            if I were less insecurely certain, too;
    the colleagues I work with,
        yet of whom I'd be less wary
            if friendship meant as much as power and status;
    the enemies,
        those become now faceless names and nameless faces,
            all those who enrage and frighten me,
                yet might not if I listened more
                    and needed less to win, be right and blameless.
And I bring, as well,
    the lonely and lost,
        the battered and broken,
            the oppressed and addicted,
                the sick and grief-stricken.
Here they all are with me,
    on my conscience,
        in my heart,
            as I must be in yours,
                please God.
So, by grace,
    would I pray us
        home.

The narrow way of trust

Lord, give me courage
    to confront myself honestly,
        shuck the pretense, strip to the real;
    to act justly with those close to me,
        advocate justice for those at some remove;
    to work to heal what is injured in my life
        and celebrate the wondrous rest.
O God, lead me in the narrow way of trust
    for wide is the way of distrust,
        painful the destruction it twists to.
Lighten the baggage I load on myself and others
    when I behave as though I were surer of my choices
        than I am, or can ever be.
Ease my anxiety about being wrong or exposed as a fool,
    for I am always at least a little of both
        and all the more when I deny I am either.
Deepen my trust
    that together we can unravel the snarls of my life,
        the knots I tie myself into,
    that, so relieved, I might help untie
        the knots I tie others into.
Then go with me into awe or ache so deep
    I am forced to sort out what matters,
        and to be buoyed by it,
            in this illusion-flooded world.
Empower me
    to be a bold participant,
        rather than a timid saint in waiting,
            in the difficult ordinariness of now;
    to exercise the authority of honesty,
        rather than to defer to power,
            or deceive to get it;
    to influence someone for justice,
        rather than impress anyone for gain;
    and, by grace, to find treasures
            of joy, of friendship, of peace
                hidden in the fields of the daily
                    you give me to plow.

A CHANCE

It had been an ugly day. Kevin Warner lay in bed, one fist under his pillow, the other pressed against the acid burning in his chest. He felt bereft and wished, as he often did, that he could pray toward some kind of ease. He tried to find a word to begin the effort again. He managed "God," "maybe," and "help" before he found himself distracted by the pattern of the street light on the bedroom walls. For a few moments he stared at the patterns. Then he lost interest.

"Damn it," he hissed through clenched teeth, "goddamn bad days hang on like pit bulls. Takes half the night to pry them off. But good days slip away like trout you can't catch, a flash of silver and they're gone. Where the hell's the justice in that? Or the mercy?" A passing car sent a flash flood of light across the wall. "Hope I die fast, of a heart attack or something, not some bitchin' thing that goes on for frigging ever."

He rolled over, trying to relieve the ache in his back. He thought of the therapist he'd seen for a few sessions — at his first wife's insistence. He'd been angry when the guy had suggested that the problem might be in *him*, from his past, not so much in his first wife's behavior, or in whatever was going on around him; that maybe what was wrong wasn't some malicious virus invading from someone else's sneeze, but something in himself, some perverse blindness or deafness or something. Why him? Why his fault? The hell with that. He'd tossed the idea out as being too introspective, too self-preoccupied, no solution to the situation he found himself in. Plus, the idea that his first wife was somehow getting off scot-free made him angry. He'd always thought of problems as being like equations involving an X: an unknown but objective factor that had to be identified in order for there to be a solution.

But maybe the shrink had been right, and he'd been too stupid to see that he was the X, or too proud to admit that he was. Anyway, back then he'd resisted the whole idea of therapy. And after the divorce happened, and his life improved, it didn't seem to matter. Yet recently it began to occur to him that maybe there was some buried guilt around the divorce or something that was making him feel so angry, so defeated, so humiliated now. Whatever was going on, self-doubt nagged at him. He worried about his health, his abilities, his attractiveness. What was the matter?

He realized that he was sweating. He sat up and looked at the clock radio. One o'clock in the damn morning. His stepdaughter, Jody, wasn't in yet. "Jesus," he thought, "she's just eighteen, and she acts like she's twenty-five, for God's sake." He'd come to think of stepchildren as land mines in the terrain of remarriage. You had to be so damn careful where you stepped if you wanted to keep things from exploding. Claire, his wife, had told him that Jody would be home from the party around midnight. "Okay, it's one o'clock," he muttered, "Where is she? And why isn't Claire upset, awake, worrying?"

Anger began a slow burn in him, but then fear partially doused it. He checked off the possibilities. Maybe Jody had an accident with the car. Maybe some guy was talking her into having sex, and she'd end up pregnant or get AIDS. Maybe she was doing drugs — coke or crack or ice or whatever. Drugs petrified him. If there were drugs at the party, who knows what would happen to Jody. "Kids just go along," he growled under his breath, running a hand through his hair and noticing that it felt thinner than ever. That realization broke the spell. "Come on," he told himself, "get hold of yourself. Why do you always think the worst? Jody's probably fine. Besides, it's really up to Claire, and she's not worrying."

He looked over at Claire. She was breathing in a slow, even cadence. Her hair spilled over her cheek and across her pillow, hair dark as mystery itself, the few silver strands only enhancing it. Women were always mysterious to him, alluring yet a little frightening. He thought of his mother: Her practiced grace and religious demeanor had been both irresistible and manipulative, while she herself had remained emotionally inaccessible. Her expectations of him, as well as the rules of their relationship, had never been openly discussed, only vaguely alluded to and casually assumed. The assumptions had then been either verified or broken by his behavior. Her corresponding responses of pride or hurt, echoed by his father, had felt dangerous and confusing to him. He'd tended to withdraw into anger and anxiety — and loneliness.

Now he studied Claire. Sleep seemed to accentuate her beauty. A sudden sexual urge roused in him, an urgent desire to take her, hard, quick, not make love but just be crudely physical, primitive, release his tension, meet a need. Then, as quickly as it had come, the urge cooled in his guilty awareness of how impersonal and exploitative, almost violent, his urge was. That frightened him. Did he want to hurt Claire somehow? He didn't think so, but that the question had even occurred to him was disturbing.

He and Claire had been married eight years, had been friends but not lovers for several years before that. Whatever the reasons for their first marriages — the hunger for sex or security, or simply acting out their families' scripts — they'd been painful mistakes for everyone. The divorces had intensified and made public the frustration, emptiness, and fruitless conflicts that had taken on such stupefying weight over the years. He was sorry for all of it, but deeply grateful to be with Claire now. With Claire, the conflicts were not fruitless.

Yet, looking at her, Kevin was aware that it had been a long time since he'd really noticed how beautiful she was or really even seen her at all. A longing stirred in him, a nostalgia. They had gone through so much in order to be together. He was shocked to realize how many months it had been since he'd felt close to her or confided in her. It was as if everything between them had become perfunctory, functional; they were just keeping things running smoothly for the kids as well as themselves and their careers.

Claire's daughter, Jody, lived with them all the time except for some holidays and a month in the summer when she was with Claire's first husband, Newton, and his wife, both of whom traveled much of the time in their jobs. Kevin's seventeen-year- old son, Nate, and his thirteen-year-old daughter, LuAnn, alternated months between living with him and Claire and his first wife, Betsy. There were rough spots, land mines, but no major disasters. Claire's career as an interior designer was going very well; his in advertising was less exciting but okay. They paid the bills, met their social obligations. "Obligations," he thought, "good God, what a way to think of them. What's happening to us?"

He stood up and rubbed his neck. He recalled the chill he sometimes felt when he saw older couples in restaurants, eating their dinners in joyless silence, drowning in their lonely privacies, bound only by resignation to the repetition of the years, too weary or scared to risk anything different. He'd vowed that would never happen to him. But was it beginning? Even to him and Claire? Did it happen inevitably, to everyone — people just slipping into relational black holes? He shuddered.

He reached for his watch on the night table, padded over to the window, and checked the time by the street light. One fifteen. Where the hell was Jody? Surely she knew they'd be worried. Didn't kids think about anyone but themselves? Claire always defended Jody whenever he criticized her. Those exchanges always seemed to escalate into arguments about which of them was guilty of what or jealous of whom. Then they'd reach a limit of what either could bear and settle into a kind of workable truce for the time being. What was his anger really about? After the arguments, he felt isolated and lonely, as he did now.

He went out into the hallway and downstairs to the kitchen. He poured himself a glass of milk and sat down at the kitchen table. The milk tasted faintly sour. He emptied it out in the sink, washed out the glass, put in some ice, sloshed on some bourbon, thought about his heartburn and shrugged. He took his drink into the living room, sat down in the darkness, and took a long swallow. He slouched down in the chair, stretched his legs out, and idly noticed that the street light patterns reflected mostly on the living room floor rather than on the walls, as they did in the bedroom.

That struck him as profound somehow, something he should write a poem about.

He groped for a word, an idea to start, but couldn't. He took another swallow of bourbon. Maybe the drink would help him to sort out all the thoughts that were chasing their tails around in his brain.

He found himself staring at the street light patterns on the floor, sipping his drink. After a few moments, he pulled his legs in and leaned forward. "*Soft light,*" he began composing his poem, "no, *insistent light. Insistent, unassuming light . . . pulling back . . .* that's too strong . . . *tugging, brushing,* ahh, *brushing back the . . . the curtain . . . the veil of night . . .* yes . . . *brushing back the veil of night to . . .* to what? *To show . . .* no, *to reveal the . . . the tantalizing sight of . . .* of what? Oh, Christ, I'm getting maudlin."

It had begun while he was waiting for the seven forty-five train that morning. Roland Brooks, a young black who'd joined his advertising agency, Knapp, Kline, Powell and Row, as a copywriter a couple of years ago came up to him on the platform as he was checking the sports page.

"Hey, Kevin." Roland's off-handed greeting was transparent disguise of his intentional approach.

"Hey, man," he replied, sticking out his hand for their ritual brothers' handshake. Roland ignored it. Kevin felt angry but careful. "What's happenin'? Never saw you riding the train before," Kevin continued.

"Yeah, usually car pool it. Cheaper. But today my pool didn't work out. Too many complications." Roland's smile was enigmatic.

He decided to ignore Roland's barb. "Well TGIF, right? How's it going otherwise?"

"Passable," Roland answered. "By the way, congratulations on landing the Brenman assignment. Juicy job."

"Yeah, thanks." He felt wary, waiting for Roland's other shoe to drop.

Roland tilted his head back slightly and the words came rushing out, rehearsed, urgent, just slightly louder than a whisper. "Look, Kevin, I'm proud, so this is hard to ask; but I want to work on the Brenman assignment with you. I've got some good ideas. You could ask Ollie to make me your assistant on the project. It would break the stereotype of me at Knapp, Kline and give me a chance. Professionally." Roland smiled.

Roland's request caught him completely off guard. His reply was louder than it had to be. "What are you talking about, man? I can't just go to Ollie and ask for something like that. I mean, why? You gotta be kidding."

"I'm not kidding," Roland answered. "I'm asking you because you're the guy who's always talkin' the brothers' talk and shakin' the brothers' handshake. Okay, let's see if you can walk the brothers' walk, as they say. Just ask Ollie to assign me to the project."

His stomach tightened and his upper lip began sweating. "What is this, a test, Roland? Why would Ollie listen to me? What would I be selling, a black copywriter who wants a shot? Won't wash, man. He'd think I'd gone over the edge."

Roland's words came through gritted teeth, "And there we have it, don't we? All you really know about me is that I'm a black guy working at Knapp, Kline as a lowly copywriter, someone you can show off your brothers' handshake with to prove how liberal and open you are. That's it, right?"

He glanced away. "Damnit, Roland, get off my back. What am I supposed to know about you? What did you ever tell me? Now you're asking me for an enormous favor just because you're black?"

Roland bore in. "No. I want the job because I'd be good at it, and you could use me. I want the job because I didn't get it because I'm black."

"What the hell are you talking about, Roland?" He kept wishing the train would come.

Roland turned, spit, sighed and said softly, "What you don't know about me is that I know something about the advertising business. Studied it in college. Worked at it before this job. What you don't know abut me is that I have both the talent and the guts to risk putting a proposal together for the Brenman deal, that I'd worked after hours on my own to do it. You just know that I should be grateful to be one of the copywriters. Well, I'm not. So I made a damn good presentation to Ollie and the committee. But they wouldn't even let me make my proposal to Brenman as an option. You had the assignment all the way. And that is how the world works, as if you didn't know."

He felt defensive. "Hey man, I'm sorry it happened that way. But you gotta know Ollie's turned me down a few times, too. And hell, I've been with the firm a few years."

"And you're white," Roland nodded, the flicker of a smile shaded with anger crossing his face.

Suddenly Kevin grabbed Roland's arm and his words bristled. "I think talent was the major factor in my getting the assignment, Roland, whether you like it or not."

"Let go of my arm, please!" Roland said with menacing evenness. After a face-saving moment of staring at Roland, Kevin let go. Roland continued, "Talent? Yes, but is that ever enough? This is your chance to become a partner, isn't it? Could lose it just as easy, though. I can help you. Believe me. If you've got the guts to let me."

Kevin heard the train approaching behind him. He didn't know what to say.

Roland put a hand on his arm and, just loud enough for him to hear over the hiss of the train's brakes and the rush of the commuters for the cars, said very precisely, "Look, I won't be in today. But I'll see you at the office Monday. Please, think about what I said."

Kevin had watched nonplused as Roland walked up the stairs, out of the station. Finally, he had turned to get on the train himself, just as it was pulling out of the station.

The train had been crowded and he'd had to stand all the way. When he got to the office, he'd had one of those dull, all-day headaches.

With a start, Kevin realized that he had lost track of how long he'd been staring at the patterns on the living room floor. Quickly he stood, swished the bourbon and ice around in his glass, took a swallow, and walked to the window. One forty-two a.m.

Saturday morning and still no sign of Jody. Maybe he should call the home where the party was. No, even if he knew where the hell it was, that would only embarrass Jody. Or maybe it would just embarrass him. He'd have to check with Claire first, anyway. Maybe he ought to check with the police, discreetly, without creating a fuss. But how the hell could he be discreet with the cops? What would he say?

He shrugged, put down his glass, and decided to check on the other kids. He went upstairs, running his hand over the banister, the feel of the wood like an old friend, comforting. He stood for a moment looking at his thirteen-year-old, LuAnn. The blanket was half off, dragging on the floor, exposing the awkwardly beautiful neck and shoulder, and long, lazily curved back and swelling hip of his sleeping daughter. He retrieved the blanket, tucked it around her.

She opened her eyes. "Oh, it's you, Daddy."

He whispered, "Who did you think it was, honey?" He meant to be tender but sounded gruff. He wanted to say something more, but she had already gone back to her interrupted dreams.

He leaned on the post at the foot of the bed and watched her, his love for her filling in the silence. He recalled how excited she'd been about a dance last weekend. She was going on her first date with some young boy she described as "awesome." But the date had turned sour, and she'd cried as she told him and Claire how her date was a "dweeb" who'd "totally bagged her" for his "butt-breath, buddies" and how males were "shmeg-brained roadkill" she'd never have anything to do with again.

He'd listened sympathetically but realized how helpless he was to protect her from her youthful vulnerability that would inevitably lead to her disillusionment, her growing-up discovery that pain and defeat were as much a part of life as delight. He pondered the curious mix of wisdom and bitterness that the discovery would generate in her and wondered which portion would be the greater. So much of her life would depend on whether wisdom won out over bitterness. He wondered what he had done, or might yet do, to tilt the scale one way or the other. He wondered which was the weightier in him. His eyes teared, and he turned away and left the room.

He walked slowly down the hall to Nate's room. Nate slept like he did everything else: full steam, totally immersed — feet sticking out one side of the bed, one arm wrapped around a pillow, the other dropped off the edge, oddly bent against the floor. He slept oblivious in a sea of pants, socks, shirts, sweaters, jockey shorts, T-shirts, sneakers, soccer shoes, uniforms, and school books, all cast-off, wadded, crumbled, stuffed in all directions by this seventeen-year-old hurricane who, no matter which way he was thrown, or threw himself, always seemed to land on his feet.

Kevin shook his head, leaned over, picked up a couple of unidentifiable pieces of clothing from the floor, and banged his head on an open bureau drawer, which, in reflex of rage, he slammed shut.

Nate lifted his head, muttered, "Hey, wh'zup, man?" and collapsed back on his pillow.

Kevin rubbed his throbbing head and in a whisper as close to a shout as he could manage, he answered, "Damnit, Nate, when are you going to clean up this room, for God's sake?"

Nate's head jerked up again, as though it were yanked by some giant puppeteer, and he mumbled, "Clean? Oh yeah, soon . . . not now. Can't see. T'morrow f'sure. You c'n help me t'morrow, okay?" Before Nate's head hit the pillow, he was asleep again.

In the dim light Kevin checked his own head for blood and stood looking at his blissful son. He'd just been summarily dismissed, but he felt like laughing. He remembered how disgusted he used to be when his own father would say, ad nauseum, that it all went by too fast. But his father had been right. There was little Nate stretched out, big-footed, bass-voiced, smelling slightly of after shave. Nate had been only nine years old when the divorce took place and the bi-monthly shifts between homes had begun. Kevin wondered now if he'd been so wrapped up in Claire, and his career, that he hadn't been as attentive to Nate as he should have.

He wondered if it would have been better for Nate, and for LuAnn, if their mother and he hadn't divorced. Even the thought sent a shiver through him. It would have been worse, much worse, he was sure. But that didn't mean the divorce hadn't caused some damage to them, either. But what? How much? Didn't his own happiness with Claire compensate for at least some of the damage? He had never talked with Nate about much of it. His own father had never talked to him about such matters, either. His parents had always acted as though everything was fine between them, even when he knew it wasn't. The pretense of that was depressing to him. Maybe he should talk to Nate. What would he say? What would he ask? The idea was appealing, and frightening, too. He pulled the sheet over Nate's feet and left the room.

He made his way back downstairs, feeling very old. One fifty-eight a.m. and no Jody. He sat down in the upholstered rocker Claire had gotten him for his fortieth birthday six years ago as sort of a joke. They'd laughed about it then. Now, he felt like he belonged in it. But he wondered where he really *did* belong. What had happened over the years? Who'd bought him, used him, shaped him? No, that wasn't it. Whom had he *let* buy, use, shape him — and for what? So far, what did his life add up to? What did he really want? Questions, questions, suddenly all these questions. He put his head back, and his mind sniffed back to the meeting he'd had that afternoon with Ollie.

Ollie Row, world-class scum bag, President of Knapp, Kline, Powell and Row because he happened to be the son of one of the founders. Ollie was old money, private school, Ivy League, and only four years older than he. Ollie's charm attracted customers but repelled people who worked very long for him and corroded whatever creative gifts he might once have had. The standard line of office black humor was the comment that someone had "caught the charm," which meant any variation from being conned to conning.

Still, Knapp, Kline was a good advertising agency, and Kevin had worked to be one of its top account execs and its expert in major media ads. But he wasn't a partner and it ate at him. More than once he'd felt twinges of envy toward Ollie, even though he knew that Ollie had become less a man than a commercial for whatever the good life was at the moment, a person for whom truth was reduced to what could fit into a catchy slogan, and for whom human beings were, or ideally should become, consumers of sweet smells, bright colors, sleek cars that would actually transform their lives. The trouble was that Ollie expected everyone who worked for him to hold the same view. But for Kevin, at the end of the day, it all seemed to boil down to the fact that Ollie was successful, he wasn't.

Ollie had called just before lunch. "Kevin, I know you're probably very busy, but I'd appreciate it if you could arrange to see me at two this afternoon. I need your advice about the Poley account."

He'd told Ollie he'd be there, took some aspirin, and left the office for a walk. Why the Poley account? What did Ollie want?

At two, he'd gone in to see Ollie. Ollie had turned on the charm and, after a few minutes of chatter, Kevin had been thoroughly uncomfortable and on guard. What was Ollie after? Then it came.

"I presented the layout to the Poley people," Ollie said. "They liked what I'd done. They signed the contract and gave us the go ahead. They want to have it on the networks and to the mag people by early next month."

He felt angry. "Well, congratulations on what *you've* done, Ollie? Funny, but I thought it was what *we'd* done. I even thought I heard talk about a bonus for some of us."

"Oh, Kevin, Kevin. Why are you so touchy? Of course, a lot of us worked on it, you most of all. In-house, we know where the credit belongs, and a bonus, too, on the slim chance there'll be one. But you know how clients are. Clients like dealing with me because I'm President. My name's the firm name. So I presented it that way. Surely you'd agree that what matters is that the deal gets done. Right?"

He felt he'd been had. "So what you wanted to talk to me about was my not getting any bonus. Is that it?" He started to get up.

Ollie held up his hand, smiling. "No, no. I knew that wouldn't matter much to you after I gave you the Brenman assignment."

He was on the edge of his chair, looking at the carpet, not trusting himself to look at Ollie. "*Gave* me? I thought I earned the Brenman assignment."

Ollie looked grieved. "Of course you did. That goes without saying. Why are you so testy, Kevin? Relax. I expect you to do very well with the Brenman job. You got the job because so much rides on it. For all of us. Now are we on the same page?"

The man was damned clever. With an easy smile and quick feint, Ollie had wiped out his bonus, pointed out his indebtedness, and turned up the screws on the Brenman job. Kevin slumped back in his chair. "Same page, Ollie. So what did you want to talk to me about?"

Ollie stood and walked to his conference table. "I really want to consult with you on the Poley account since you'll be working it out from this point. I want to tell you of a change I made in the approach. Come to an understanding. Here, look." Ollie motioned him over, and reluctantly he moved to Ollie's side of the table as Ollie began talking and pointing to the layouts.

"The theme's going to be 'If Love touches you, you can touch anyone.' I'm excited about it. It's simple and just suggestive enough. We'll run it with pictures of beautiful women, handsome men adoring them, different locations, you know. Overlay it with a bottle of the Love perfume, or show the bottle somewhere in the picture. At the bottom of the page, or the end of the spot, we add the words 'Love by Poley.' Like it?"

Kevin stared at the layouts. What was there about Ollie that made him feel his manhood had been snipped off before he'd realized it? "Ollie," he said at last, "that theme. Don't you think its just a little excessive?" He glanced at Ollie.

Ollie looked smug. "It's your line, Kevin. You dropped it and all I did was pick it up again. I'm surprised you don't like it."

Kevin massaged his eyes with his thumb and fingers. "Ollie, I dropped the line because I came up with it in a brainstorming session without really thinking about it. After we'd run it by once or twice, I realized it makes love out to be a commodity you get at a department store."

Ollie frowned and said softly, "Kevin, that's advertising and you know it. It's a business. It's more than that, it's politics, it's education, it's religion. It gets people to buy your product, and that's what makes the world go around. If wearing this perfume makes a woman feel better about herself, it's done its job."

Kevin turned to face Ollie. "But you have to admit it's manipulative, Ollie. It manipulates by twisting around one of the most . . . honored words we have. It's like saying, 'Love works if you work it right.' Some lonely waitress out in Keokuk is going to save up her tips for a month and buy a bottle of 'Love' hoping, even against her better judgment, that a few well-placed splashes of it will enable her to touch the 'anyone' of her dreams, wrap him up, and live happily ever after. But it isn't so. Sooner or later she'll find that out. What about that waitress, Ollie? She's the reason I dropped that line."

Ollie looked disappointed. "Kevin, Kevin, nothing much is going to help that waitress, and 'Love,' even if it comes in a bottle, isn't going to hurt her much either. What are these sudden doubts you're having? How can I be confident you're up to the Brenman job with these kinds of reservations? Maybe you've just had a bad day. I'll chalk it up to that. So, let's just say I liked your theme for the Poley deal, and they bought it. So take the layouts and work your magic. If you have a problem, let me know."

Kevin wanted to say "No," but he was afraid. Ollie was warning him about the Brenman account. He could lose it, maybe even lose his job. He knew the world was full of bright guys on his heels — guys like Roland. Besides, maybe Ollie was right, maybe there wasn't really a good reason not to do what the client decides they want done. Maybe his own anger, or envy, or whatever, was clouding his judgment. So, he said, quietly, "It has been a bad day, Ollie. You know I'll do it, and you know I'll handle the Brenman job well." The idea of asking Ollie about making Roland his assistant on the Brenman job flitted across his mind, but he knew the timing was lousy. He also realized he'd ask Ollie later about Roland joining him to work on the Brenman project.

"I'll get things rolling." He turned for the door.

Ollie interrupted his exit. "Kevin, I really do appreciate what you do. You are magic with layout. And a superb copywriter."

Kevin scarcely was able to push the words through the rage that constricted his throat. "Copywriter, Ollie? Christ! Is that all I am to you? A *copywriter*?"

Ollie was smiling, but it obviously was a put down, a rapier thrust. "Kevin, I'm just saying you write like Yeats, for heaven's sake. We all write copy here. Take it as the compliment I meant."

He couldn't get Ollie in focus. He gulped and said, hoarsely, "Sure, Ollie, sure. Thanks." His own smile was a sickly imitation of Ollie's. He turned and left Ollie's office. "Copywriter?" he muttered all the way back to his office.

For the rest of the afternoon, he had sulked in his office, wasting time, which had made him feel even worse.

Even now, some twelve hours later, Kevin could feel the anger still churning. He rocked slightly in the shadowy living room and began talking aloud to himself, "Why do I give a damn? It all seems so . . . phony . . . Ollie, me . . . everything . . . Maybe all you can do is cover up . . . color up . . . the ugliness and . . . compromise . . . love's just . . . an illusion . . . a good sell. 'If love touches you . . .' What the hell . . . write . . . a poem about it . . . someday. Copywriter . . . copy . . ."

 His head snapped forward. He must have dozed. A car door was slamming. Jody! He looked at his watch. Quarter after two. He got up, walked into the kitchen, and switched on the low counter lights just as Jody came in.

Jody looked startled. "Kevie, what are you doing up?"

"Where did you think I'd be with you out this late? Where the hell have you been!" It was the same the tone his father had used on him as a boy. He flinched at the sound of it.

"At the party." Jody leaned against the counter, a wary defiance on her face.

"You were supposed to be home at midnight," he growled. "Why weren't you?"

Jody smiled tentatively. "You want an honest answer or a diplomatic one?"

He didn't dare return her smile or he'd lose his advantage. "You're two hours and fifteen minutes late and in no position to make jokes."

Jody's smile disappeared. "Okay, Kevie, here's the straight answer, but I don't think you're going to like it. I didn't come home because I didn't want to. None of the other kids were leaving, and I wanted to stay. Does that satisfy you?"

He tried to control his temper. "Why didn't you call? Didn't we deserve a call? Didn't you know we'd worry?"

Jody met his eyes and said with an effort that up-pitched her voice, "I knew if I called, you'd just make me come home. I think I'm old enough to make my own decisions about some things. I'm a responsible person."

His anger boiled over and he yelled, "Old enough to decide what? To break your word? To ignore other people? To make them sick with worry? Who the hell is ever old enough to do that?"

"I didn't mean that," Jody yelled back, tears rolling down her cheeks. "I meant I'm old enough to be responsible for some of my own decisions."

"Christ," he snorted. He felt dizzy. He pulled out a chair and sat down at the table. At the quiet core of his anger was the nagging suspicion that there might be some truth to what Jody was saying, and he felt an oddly unexpected pride as she stood there challenging him. He'd never stood up to his own father, who had always made him feel so wrong that he'd ended up not even liking himself. He didn't stand up to Ollie. To anyone. Even to Claire. Maybe he was on the way to ending up like those silent old people in restaurants. "God help me," he thought, tracing the flow pattern on the tablecloth in the soft light.

He looked at Jody, standing there, waiting for his reply. Tears came to his eyes and he looked down at his hands. What the hell was that line he'd learned in Sunday School, something about the sins of the fathers passing on to the children unto the third and fourth generations? Damn if those old Jews didn't know what they were talking about. But how could he stop it? Why couldn't good stuff go from fathers to children? Or even better, from children to fathers? Crazy.

"Look, Jody," he began tensely, unaware that Claire had heard them yelling and was standing in the doorway, "the point is, I was afraid something had happened to you."

"Okay, I'm sorry. I should have called you," Jody blurted out. "You're right about that. But I didn't want to come home and don't see why I should have to. There's no school tomorrow. Why should I have to be home at twelve?"

"That's what the yelling's about?" Claire asked softly.

Claire's voice startled him. He jerked around. "Damn, you scared me. I didn't realize you'd . . ." He waved his hand uncertainly. "Sorry about the yelling. Jody just came in and, yeah, that's what it was about," he answered. He looked back at Jody. "I don't know, Jody, maybe you shouldn't have had to be in by twelve. But why didn't you talk about it *before* you left? You never talk about anything with me." He sat heavily.

"I don't know. You're not home much, for one thing." Jody was lining the toe of her shoe on a crack between the kitchen floor tiles. "And I didn't think you'd want to listen." She raised her eyes to him. "And it's always so one way. You never talk about yourself, what's going on with you. You just want *me* to talk, or you just want to tell me stuff you're afraid about for me. What about *you*, Kevie?"

"I wish you wouldn't call me that," he said, surprising himself. "It sounds like the name of that bird that can't fly." He could see that Jody was startled by his request.

"I've always called you that," she protested. "I'll stop if you want. What should I call you?"

"Try 'Kevin.' Okay? And I talk about things I'm afraid of for you because I care about you. Things happen to kids. You might get hurt."

"I'm not exactly a kid anymore," Jody replied levelly. "And I know about things."

He stood up and leaned against the other end of the counter, not facing her. "Jody, knowing about things and not getting hurt by them aren't the same. You're young. Maybe your judgment isn't always as good as you think. About drinking. Or driving. About drugs. That things kill you. And sex. There's AIDS out there, and herpes and who knows what. Damn right, I'm afraid for you."

"And how many times have you said all this to me? Don't you think I'm responsible? Can't you trust me?" Jody's tone was exasperated.

"How do I know?" he countered, raising his voice. "Coming in late like this doesn't help much."

"Okay," she conceded, "I said I was sorry. How many times do I have to say that? Or prove myself to you? Really, haven't I earned your trust by now? Forget tonight. No, don't forget it. At least I've been honest with you about it. And I've never come home drunk, or driven when I drink. Sure, I drink a little. Beer mostly. But I think I'm just as responsible as you about drinking. And believe me, I don't do drugs. I'm not stupid. I am trustworthy. But there's one thing you should know: I'm not a virgin anymore. You might as well know that."

"Oh, Jesus," he uttered, sinking down onto the chair. "Don't tell me."

Jody rushed on. "But I am telling you. And I'm telling you I'm still responsible. I'm on the pill. I don't sleep with just anyone. I know you're scared and so am I. And I'll tell you what I'm scared of. Sure, AIDS is part of it. But I'm even more scared about being so scared that I miss my life. I don't want to live like I'm in one of those plastic bubbles kids have to stay in when they can't risk being exposed to any diseases. So, yes, I think about 'things,' Kevin. Long and hard. There, I've talked. Your turn."

He felt angry and frightened. He looked at Claire. She was calm. "You knew all this?" he asked. "About the sex and . . . everything?"

Claire nodded. "Yes."

"You never said anything to me," he protested.

"We haven't talked much lately," she said, putting a hand on his shoulder. "Besides, Jody and I agreed that it was her place to tell you. Now she has. I think that's good. But, Jody, it's not all right for you to come in this late. Kevin's right. You should have talked to us about it before."

"I know, Mom." Jody sounded contrite and tired. "Can we just go to bed now, please?"

He was still trying to grasp what was happening. "Jody, I'm . . . you said it was my turn to talk, but I'm not sure what to say. I love you, and I . . . I'm still scared about AIDS, for one thing. The pill doesn't help with that. And . . ." his voice trailed off.

Jody walked over to him, put her hand over Claire's hand on his shoulder. "Kevin, the sex has been with one guy. Scott. You met him. I know we're young, but we're careful. We think we love each other, but . . . I don't know if you can understand this but somehow the sex thing got in the way of our finding out more about our love because sex kind of dominated everything until we could get it out of the way and see what else there was between us. Mom said it was like that for her and Dad, so they got married. But look at the disaster that was. Scott and I didn't want that. So we did it this way. Can you understand? It just seems the most . . . moral, the . . . best option for us right now. Okay?"

"I don't know," he sighed, his hands massaging his brow. "Maybe it is." He thought about him and Betsy getting married so young, mainly for sex. "Maybe."

There was silence for a moment. Then Claire said, "It's late. Bedtime." She and Jody hugged briefly and Jody left, touching his arm on the way past. Claire watched her, then turned to him and asked softly, "Coming?"

"In a minute," he answered. "Go ahead. I'll be right there." He listened to her climb the stairs. He pushed himself up slowly, walked to the switch, and turned the light off. Leaning against the sink, he stared out the window. After a moment he realized he was staring at a something in the yard. He squinted, saw it was a plastic ball from one of the neighbors' kids. The street light made the ball look like a little UFO, one part in the shadow, the other reflecting the street light. The illusion it created made his yard, his world look strangely unfamiliar. Who was the alien? Was it him? Was it the world? He turned away from the window. "Lord have mercy," he muttered, shuffling across the floor. He felt overwhelmingly tired. Using the banister, he pulled himself up the stairs.

When he reached the top, he turned toward Jody's room, approached, and knocked on the door.

"Yes?" Jody responded.

He pushed open the door and stepped in, hand still on the knob. He smiled tentatively. "Jody . . . I'd like to ask you something."

Jody was sitting on the edge of her bed with the headphones of her stereo over her ears. She took them off. "Sure."

He felt embarrassed. "What are you listening to?" he asked.

"Streisand," she answered. "Old tape. Don't know why I dug it out. Felt like something, you know, different, I guess."

"I like her, too," he said. He gazed around the room. "Look, I'm not sure about . . . what just happened. But, I think you said something about having earned my trust. You think trust has to be earned, right?"

Jody nodded, "Yeah."

"Well," he went on, "I agree but . . . how do we do that? I mean, how do I do that? With you?"

Jody crossed her legs, put one arm back on the bed and leaned into it. "I guess we could start by being honest. I mean, about what's really going on, you know. You telling me straight what you're actually thinking or feeling, about being scared or happy, stuff like that . . . that would make me feel closer to you, trust you. You never do that, so it's like you don't trust me, and then I don't do it 'cause it's like I learned not to trust you, either. See, in the past when I've told you stuff about me — a little, anyway — you've always given me advice, which makes me mad and makes me feel I'm wrong for being the way I am. I wish I knew how it is for you. I need that. I mean, from a man, too." There were tears in her eyes. "You know?"

He leaned against the wall. "That's different from what I learned to do," he said, his voice breaking slightly, "or how it was for me growing up. Maybe I can learn. I'd like to be close. I'd like to trust . . . and be trusted."

He felt a tear roll down his cheek, and he felt that he should stop. But he didn't. "I learned to put the face on things I thought my parents wanted. And my friends, my boss. My parents made me feel guilty about sex, afraid. I still am, sometimes. I don't know much about trust. For me, there were strict rights and wrongs. Still are, I guess. I hid my wrongs. So when you talk about sex, I get . . . anxious. I'm not sure I'm entirely off the wall about it, but maybe I am, some. I guess I am. I hope we can, maybe, change things."

Jody stood as if she were going to come to him but then seemed to change her mind. She just stayed there with an open expression on her face and looked directly into his eyes. Very softly she said, "We've got a chance, Kevin. We really do." Their eyes held, and there was an ease in their smiles. Then she whispered, "Thanks. Would you turn the light out now? I've really had it for today."

He switched off the light and backed out, aware of the faint beat of the music and the small lights on the stereo dial, like the night lights he remembered leaving on in his kids' rooms when they were small.

The tears continued down his cheeks as he padded down the hall to his own room. The lamp on the night table was on, and Claire was awake. He began to laugh, a very easy, small laugh. Without a word he turned off the light, laid down, leaning on one arm, putting the other over Claire.

Then it broke through him, the sound and the shaking, though whether laughter or sobbing he wasn't sure, only that it was all right. "O God, we've got a chance," he managed to gasp, "I've . . . got a chance." His head came down on the pillow, his body trembling with the small, quiet tremors of a storm as it passed. "You . . . me . . . O God . . . a . . . chance . . . tomorrow." And then he was asleep, with a smile trickling lopsidedly off his face onto the pillow.

Claire turned and looked at him for a moment. "Yes, tomorrow," she whispered, kissing his forehead lightly. A small smile eased across her lips before she closed her eyes. She hadn't noticed the flicker of the street light on Kevin's foot where it splayed from the sheet at the corner of the bed.

The rustle of angels

God of thunderous silence,
deliver me from words
    that gush, but slake no thirst,
        that charm, but scour no truth,
            that seduce, but conceive no intimacy;
hush me to quietness
    to hear the rustle of angels
        in the unaffected laughter and tears of others,
            and myself;
    and be stunned to awe
        by others' simply inexplicable being-there-ness,
            their bodies, breathing, eye-lit-mystic beauty,
        and by mine.
Ease me, Unhurried One,
    into the depths of accurate listening
        that, beneath the babble,
            I may attend to
                the pleading in others' eyes,
                the longing in their smiles,
                the loneliness in their slump,
                the fears in their curses,
                the courage in their squint,
                the wisdom in their scars,
                the joy in their timid loves,
                the faithfulness in their beginning yet again;
    that on the whispered, groaning, stammering edge
    of so much hope and need and grace
        I may begin to wrestle to
            some limp of understanding,
            some tilt of trust,
            some murmur of gratitude,
                for this not-so-minor miracle,
                    for this merely beloved all
                    of yours
                        we are.

INTEGRITY

Authentic scandal

O God of power,
    unleashed to throb
        in flaming suns and roaring seas,
            in honest words and valiant hearts,
now would I strip off
    the tired camouflage of my pretensions
        so freedom might become more than a word to me,
            integrity more than a limp ideal.
It breaks through to Legion me,
    like lightning through the clouds,
        not only that you are God
            but the kind of God you are.
"Jealous" is the word:
    seething, stubborn, pursuing Lover,
        turning things upside down,
            kicking them over,
                striking them open —
                    and me with them;
    gagging me
        on my drooling envy
            of the spangled, flaunting idols
                of status, stock-options, command;
    palsying my snug arrogance,
        which clings to half-truth
            as if it were the whole,
                and sees new truth a threat;

snickering at my proud juggling
    of some precious good
        into an ultimate one;
groaning at my easy collusion
    in converting charm into a commandment,
        niceness into an article of faith,
           avoidance into an exercise of love,
                flattery into the essence of support,
                    prudence as the way of wisdom,
                        and playing faith for a reward;
tripping up my sauntering conscience
    with the terrifying reminder
        that Christ was hardest on hypocrites.

O God,
    my illusions have dissembled me,
        cowarded me from being into seeming.
Shake me now free of lies
    with enough trust
        and cock-hearted courage
        and laughing love
as will dare, at least sometimes,
    to walk your promise,
        run your freedom,
           wing your joy,
and so become one of this world's
    whole-hearted, authentic scandals.

Roused by the prowl of grace

My need is great as hope,
    my longing, fierce as wonder,
and I stumble toward you,
    drawn by the light of your promise,
        roused by the prowl of your grace
            in the far country haunt of my soul.
Rush to embrace this prodigal me, O God.
    Listen to my still-not-trusting babble
        and help me accept my way home to you.
Save me from the shadowy, stifling folds
    of timidity,
        duplicity,
            fear,
and give me a stunning glimpse
    of some light-splattered possibility
        to race my blood
            and lump my throat.
Deliver me
    from avoidance
        of life's struggles,
    from denial
        of its pleasures,
    and from the illusion
        that they're separable.
Awe me into awareness
    that I am one of the wonderment
        of only human muddling beings,
    a mix of treachery, reverence, mercy,
        of grab, gift, gender, want, and whim
            of love, meanness, confusing views
                which roil around me, and within,
so as I would no more deny
    the holy bafflement of me,
        so would I deny no one their place
            in my heart, or yours,
                or in the just community
                    or the covenant of grace.

Deepen me, then, in wisdom that defies
        the conspiracy of privilege,
            the trap of dogmatic closure,
                the lure of biases that enslave,
        and distinguishes joy from success,
            treasure from wealth,
                meaning from busy-ness,
                    love from possession,
                        peace from comfort.
Release me from my victim's cramp
        to the discipline of freedom,
            the passion of bold choice,
                the dare of creativity,
                    the courage of an honest voice,
        and to the faithful, dicey pressing on,
            through a way I can't quite see,
                toward the home I never reach,
                    and the whole I'll only be
                        with you,
                            who, even now,
                                is pressing home to me.

Deliver me from the choke

God,
    your language is silence:
        the hum of worlds
            and mysteries,
                and spirit;
    mine is words:
        the cast I throw,
            the reel I make
                to tell and to retrieve
                    what meaning as I can.
For a moment,
    suffer my language, Lord,
        and suffer me;
    mercy me out of the snarls
        I have made of it,
            and it of me,
        by my smug pretension
            that I have cast far
                or reeled much in
                    from the vasty deeps
                      of time and spirit,
                        nature or humanity.
Deliver me from the choke
    of my exaggerations,
        twisted arguments,
            shaded rhetoric,
                tilted accusations,
    empty flatteries,
        cheap excuses,
            pompous explanations,
                hollow mercies,
    complexity hocused
        into clever simplicities,
            while meaning slips away,
    trifling you
        and shrinking me.

In the moment,
    guide me, Lord,
        to the discovery of my own authentic voice:
           the glad will to speak
              small, sustaining truths
                like numbered hairs,
                noticed sparrows,
                leavened bread
                little children,
                the "our" of you in Jesus' prayer,
      that awed by the gift of words
        to reveal and heal,
           I be committed anew to
              their poetic use,
              prophetic power,
              priestly care,
              accurate cast,
              respectful reel.
Through all moments,
    teach me, Lord,
      your language:
        that slow deciphering
          to confidence and quietness of mind,
            the silence, stars, and seas,
            the signing of mute mountains,
            the hint of seeds, breathing of wind,
            the primal thrust/receive of mate,
              fused wonder in the womb,
              glad puzzlements of born,
              strange rhythms in my living,
              intimations in the passing on;
      this bearing in, and down, and up,
        this for Christ's sake of everything,
          and bloody nothing, too,
            mysteriously uniting me
              inseparably to you;
      this all of grace,
        for which I make
          this wordless kneel of praise.

Teetered on a ridge

O God,
     elusive Presence,
          insistent Other,
draw me to the border
     where hard, large truth
          escapes soft, small certainty —
               certainly my own —
          and grows in the between of risky encounter:
                    honest speaking,
                    brave listening,
                    painful struggle
                    hard-scrabble sifting,
               in that scary, sweaty swing
                    toward those sacred others;
and I, being caught, seen,
     spun, stripped clean,
          am teetered on a ridge to see
               a different, saving view
                    I hadn't dared to see before
          where I will slowly learn
               the balance of liberating trust
          and find my authentic way,
               between loyalty
                    and flexibility,
               commitment
                    and openness,
               witness
                    and self-righteousness,
               courage
                    and self-advancement,
               quietness
                    and cowardice.

Grant me not only to tiptoe that edge
    but to live it,
        to be it —
           a glad, welcoming lurch
           toward the day of justice,
           toward the fleet bright wings of joy,
              the radiant call of beauty,
                the sear of mercy,
                a blaze of love,
                  a kingdom coming,
                    an elusively Present,
                      insistently Other,
                        saving grace
                          of you.

Fierceness churning like a sea

O God, in this search of prayer
    I discover something fierce in me
        that will not be ignored,
    and I take it as your stirring
        before my strain to ask.
It aches, this fierceness.
It screams past words, past plan,
    rising as a world to dare,
        in the contractions of rebirth,
        in the laughter of adore,
            to touch, to shape,
            to find myself within,
            and to find
                a place to reach,
                  a time to stand,
                      a God to worship wildly
              with everything at hand,
                the muck and marvel of it all,
                    the whole whatever-might-be of me.
It is your stir,
    I claim it so.
        What else ever could it be?
This fierceness churning like a sea,
    flooding my eyes with longing,
        ebbing salty down my cheeks,
            a kind of amniotic fluid
            a burning out and in,
            a crying, urgent, holy demand,
                by you of me — thus me of you —
        to stop my slide to style,
            my slink to approval,
                my slither of hypocrisy,
        and to surprise the day
            with this fierceness,
                this urge to wholeness,
                this passion for integrity,
                this no longer deniable insistence
                    that my life not be a forgery.

O God, transform this fierceness into courage
    to say what I mean,
        because it will put me at risk
            of the rigors of freedom:
                being disliked for my honesty
                    rather than liked for my deceits,
                but enabling others to count on my word,
                    as I count on yours,
                        for light and life;
    to mean what I say,
        because it will shame me
            into turning clean away
                from the small purposes
                    and comfortable lies
                        on which I have wasted my energies;
    to pioneer my way with you,
        in this brave heave of love
            toward a stranger self than I have been
              within this world you're making new;
    and so to be an heir of yours,
        claiming this foolish vocation
            of announcing Christ's returning
                and living for my own.

One difficult condition

O God of unfathomable grace,
    you seem to have no conditions
        for being with me
    yet one difficult condition
        for my being with you:
    the giving up
        of my compulsion to perfection,
            this whipping of myself
                into anxious, disappointed bits and pieces,
                    a stubble of complaints, criticisms,
                        rejections, ingratitudes;
            this proud taking more upon myself
                than I can bear,
                    or than makes me bearable,
                and scatters my life into
                    sighs, excuses, poses, tears,
                        perfectly reasonable
                            despair.
Grace, then,
    for my giving up,
        which is what faith comes down to;
    for getting this fractured self
        cemented, sealed, sighted together
            with whatever glue
                of spit and mud,
                    mercy and blood
                you have at hand,
                    and heart,
    to condition me to be with you,
        to limp and love,
            sing, scream, and pray,
                through this quite imperfect world,
                    still quite awesome and enough;
    to finding my quite mysterious way
        to life, and peace, and joy,
            my bearing cross,
                my empty tomb.

Murky depths

O God of my murky depths and glorious heights,
    here I am:
        all my ambivalence and awe,
            my churning questions,
                and unslaked thirst for you,
        my awkward grope,
            ecstatic soar,
                trudging doubt,
                    and brief lighted-hearted confidence.
Accept it all
    and enable me to accept the whole
        of my preposterous, puny, perverse,
            confusing, graceful, gifted self.
Assure me that it is all right,
    and only right at all,
        to be who I am,
            to struggle my struggles,
                dance my music,
                    embrace my triumphs;
            to suffer on my own terms,
                not those of demanding others
                    I falsely try to please,
                        mistaking their favor for yours;
        and to simply turn glad, past whine or boast,
            in becoming who I am.
Forgive me out of
    my faithless presumptions
        that what you ask of me is pretense, not truth,
            innocence, not integrity,
                certainty, not fidelity;
and forgive me into
    a deep-breathing trust
        that dares to press beyond the calculated shallows
            to the kingdom-haunted depths
                of the terribly real me,
                    and this terribly real world,
                        toward a terribly real you.

HOW SWEET THE SOUND

The more forgetful Deacon Crump became, the more angry Alice Crump became — though only a few would have guessed it. It seemed to Alice that Deacon was escaping, if not from her then at least from whatever she had to stay and endure while he wandered away from their remembered world. But the angrier Alice got, the sweeter she got, until you never heard even the slightest cross word from her. Actually, that development was just the predictable extension of the way she'd been all her life. There were some, mostly at St. James Church, who called her a saint. There were others, mostly at the VFW, who called her a martyr, often prefacing the term with an unprintable obscenity.

In any case, as things got worse, Alice simply worked harder to do what she said she'd done all her life, which was "to take care of my Deacon." Although a few discussed it privately, Alice never asked herself — at least not that anyone heard — why she'd done that all her life, or why things were working out so badly for Deacon and her now, or what she got out of taking care of him either way.

But the real mystery was that the sweeter Alice got, the more rapidly Deacon's forgetfulness advanced. But not many asked why about that either, least of all Alice. People just thought that Deacon's condition was a shame, and the only question they asked was whether he suffered from Alzheimer's disease, which some, with a shudder of apprehension for themselves, were sure he did. Others simply said Deacon was "getting senile."

"Deacon" is what people called him; nearly everyone had forgotten that his real name was Daniel. Deacon was an honorary title bestowed by usage. It went back to about the time he and Alice moved into their house thirty-five years ago, and Alice began attending St. James Church about a block away. Daniel went along occasionally but preferred staying home and reading about one of his favorite subjects — astronomy (his other hobby being skeet shooting, a rather unlikely pursuit for a city dweller, but one he managed to enjoy once in a while).

But his first love was astronomy. He was awed by the pictures of nebulae and galaxies. He was fascinated yet puzzled by the Big Bang theory scientists proposed for the beginning of creation. The closest he could come to picturing it was that it must have been a gigantic version of those tiny glowing dots hurled skyward by Roman candles that suddenly burst into incredible patterns of color during fireworks displays.

"Can you imagine it," he'd mutter to himself as much as to Alice preparing lunch, "everything in the universe exploding out of something as small as a single atom?"

Alice would continue mixing the tuna fish, smile demurely, and reply, "Why, yes. It's like the Bible, Daniel. God said 'Let there be light,' and light exploded like that. And then came land and water and stars, the creation."

Daniel would chide her. "Alice, show me where it says anything about explosions in the Bible. I'll bet the word isn't even there. It doesn't say that the universe began with an explosion, now does it? Or that everything came from a single, little thing like an atom?"

With a prickly little shrug Alice would yield, giving certain words an ambiguous inflection. "Well, no, it doesn't *exactly* say that. You're right, Daniel. I'm sure the exact word isn't in the Bible. I just meant that probably it was something like an explosion when God spoke. But you're right. After all, it is difficult to imagine how an explosion could create anything."

Daniel would reply with a muted exasperation, "That's not what I meant, Alice. I mean . . . oh, it's not important." Then he'd walk around the kitchen straightening up something or other until a more harmless topic occurred to him to bring up. It was a ritual in which only the subject matter varied over the years. They lived a childless and orderly life, confined on four sides by a bridge club, a bi-monthly potluck group, a travel club, and, eventually, St. James.

For after Alice became involved in St. James, Daniel was approached in his yard one spring by the Rector, looking dapper in his tan beret. The Rector asked Daniel if he'd help take care of the church grounds because he and Alice lived so close. Daniel found himself imagining the Rector's head as a cup of cappuccino sitting on the saucer of his clerical collar, and Daniel grinned as the earnest man concluded, "Each of us is part of the body of Christ, you know, so each of us needs to contribute toward keeping that body in excellent condition."

Daniel wasn't sure just what that meant, but before he could ask, the Rector had taken Daniel's smile as assent and begun to thank him profusely. He didn't disabuse the Rector, since he liked working in the yard and really didn't mind helping out by being whatever part of the body of Christ it was that fertilized and mowed the church lawn and trimmed its bushes.

But as one Rector followed another, one thing led to another over the years, and Daniel got increasingly involved at St. James. He was asked repeatedly and never declined doing more and more: ushering, financial drives, Men's Club, Property Committee, Sunday School Treasurer, and Church Treasurer. He was even invited to be on the Music Committee because, he suspected, he didn't know much about church music and so could be the organist's "Yes" man.

Somewhere in the process of his being grafted onto "the Body," people began calling him "Deacon." No one was sure who called him that first, but in a short time everyone was calling him "Deacon." It became not only his name but his demeanor: increasingly deferential, cheerfully doing thankless tasks, his bouts of absent-mindedness being interpreted as pious detachment.

Even Alice came to call him Deacon, though she sometimes said it with an inflection that left uncertainty as to whether she intended it as a term of pride or denigration. Often, as they sat in the living room in the evening, she would look up from her paper and say, "Deacon, would you just listen to this."

He would wince at her interruption of his ball game on TV and look over at her. She would smile and proceed to read to him some item from the paper and remark, "Isn't that incredible?" using the same inflection on "incredible" as she did on "Deacon."

Her ambiguity of tone delivered him, for he felt safe in simply answering, "Yes, it is," since he was indifferent to whatever her point was and wanted only to return to his ball game, which his apparent agreement allowed him to do.

Deacon's forgetfulness grew more troublesome as the time drew near for his retirement as Comptroller of Steins, the glorified title he'd been given as office manager and accountant for the largest automobile dealership in the city. He would forget to process the paper work of some car sales. Twice he forgot to write the pay checks. He would go to St. James two or three additional times each week to do some job he'd already done. He would repeat himself, ask the same question again almost as soon as it had been answered. In exasperation someone observed, "Deacon's become like a child trying to get attention." But Deacon stubbornly refused to admit he had a problem.

One Saturday, when he was looking up the word "deactivate," which he'd read in the newspaper but thought had been misused, quite by chance he came upon the word everyone called him. It surprised him, and he began to read what the dictionary said about it. *Deacon*, he discovered, means either a second level of clergy below that of a full priest or minister, or some elected or appointed person with specific duties in the church. That definition would have been acceptable to him, but it didn't stop there. As a verb, *deacon* means to pack fruit or vegetables with only the best side showing. It also means to falsify something or doctor it up. He was surprised to find that one of the old definitions of *deacon* was to castrate a pig or some other animal. Deacon felt like a fool. He slammed the dictionary with such force that Alice jumped.

"Deacon," she exclaimed, "what's the matter, dear?"

"Nothing," he growled as he stormed out of the house, determined to walk around the block in the other direction from St. James. It was the first time he actually got lost. An hour or so after he'd left the house, Alice drove around looking for him. After another hour, she had just about decided to call the police when she spotted Deacon following a group of teen-agers into a video arcade some distance from their house. She persuaded him to come home with her, but it was only the first of the episodes that accelerated the tension between them and made Alice anxious about what she would do about Deacon.

Increasingly, Deacon became too much for Alice. He'd ask her, "Where're you going?"

"To the grocery store," she'd answer. "You stay here and read the paper like a good Deacon, and I'll bring you your favorite candy bars."

Before she'd gotten her coat on, he'd ask, "Where're you going?"

"To the store, Deacon dear. You do remember, don't you?" Then she'd go to the kitchen for her shopping list and purse.

By the time she'd got to the front door, he'd ask again, "Where are you going?"

She'd smile and say, "Oh, Deacon, I know you remember. Just relax and I'll be right back."

When she'd get back, his first question was always, "Where've you been?"

She'd sigh and give him a candy bar and tell him, "I went to the store to get you this."

One day when she got back, he was gone. She found him walking in the middle of the street in his underwear shorts, his winter overshoes, his skeet shooting jacket and hat, his shotgun over his arm, his head cocked toward the trees as if searching for birds. Another time, she got home to find him standing idly sipping a cup of tea in the middle of the kitchen while holding in his other hand the smoldering belt of his bathrobe, which she assumed had caught fire from having dangled in the burner of the stove.

When she reported these events to The Reverend T. Randolph Warren, current Rector of St. James, she was quite distraught. "Oh, Randolph, it is truly miraculous that I've happened to arrive home just in time," she exclaimed. "The good Lord must be watching out for Deacon and me. Or maybe, confused as he is, Deacon has some uncanny sense of when I'm coming home. Oh, I don't know. But what if I don't get there in time next time? I just don't know what to do, Randolph."

The Rector gave Alice the name of a practical nurse he knew, an older Irish woman who lived in the parish. Alice interviewed her and found her hourly rate was very reasonable because, as she put it, "I have a calling to serve like this." Alice nodded approvingly and, after offering her a somewhat smaller hourly rate to start, hired her on the spot. Her name was Margaret, "Maggie, for short," she said.

Shortly after Maggie came to work, Deacon's condition took on a peculiar smell that was as hard to identify as it was to miss. At first, when Alice's friends visited, they'd ask her in hushed, sympathetic voices if Deacon had become incontinent. Alice assured them he hadn't, but she didn't know what the smell was either. To mask the smell, Alice started using large amounts of her favorite lavender aerosol. After a while, Alice smelled strongly of lavender wherever she went, and on several occasions at church, her friends inquired about her new perfume, to Alice's consternation.

Indeed, Deacon's condition, and Maggie's availability, moved Alice to spend more and more time at St. James. Women there continued to touch her on the arm while smiling knowingly, thus conveying an assumed solidarity. Occasionally, they would express a mixture of encouragement and appreciation, such as "You are a model of bravery, Alice"; or "Alice, dear, you're such an inspiration to us."

The Reverend T. Randolph Warren assured her she was doing everything she could "to take care of her Deacon," that God would give her strength, and that she must keep a positive outlook. He always spoke as though he were standing in St. James' carved, elevated pulpit and often intoned to her, "You remember, of course, that St. Paul himself had a thorn in his flesh that he prayed God to remove. But God, in his wisdom, let it remain as a reminder to Paul of his need for humility and forbearance."

As Reverend Warren spoke, Alice found herself wondering what the "T." in his name stood for — perhaps Thomas, she thought, or Timothy maybe, or Theodore or . . . Turkey. She gasped. How did that ever occur to her? "God forgive me," she thought to herself, blushing visibly.

Reverend Warren paused. "Are you all right, Alice?" he inquired solicitously.

She nodded and quickly replied, "Of gobble . . . OF COURSE," she nearly shouted. "I mean, of course, I'm all right. Forgive me, I get so confused sometimes. It's just that it doesn't seem possible that my Deacon is so sinful . . . SENILE. Oh dear, I get so flustered. What I'm trying to say is that Deacon being so senile must mean I've failed somehow."

"No," the Reverend replied. "You mustn't think that. 'Whatsoever things are lovely, whatsoever things are of good report, think on these things.' That's St. Paul's counsel to us, remember? That's what you must do, Alice. God will give you strength to keep everything under control. Don't you worry."

"Thank you, Reverend," she said, "thank you. You are so kind and under-standing."

Usually, Deacon Daniel got along fairly well with Maggie, who was quite flexible in her schedule, willing to come early or stay late if needed. But occasionally Deacon would refuse to eat, or get dressed in the morning, or take a shower with Maggie lingering outside the open bathroom door to supervise. Apparently he decided that Maggie's taking that liberty gave him the right to "keep putting his hand where he shouldn't," as Maggie kept reporting it to Alice in a mildly reproving voice usually followed by a chuckle of understanding and wave of dismissal.

And there was the continual problem of getting Deacon to stay in the house and not wander around the neighborhood or go over to St. James. One Sunday morning, when Maggie was there for her agreed-upon two-hour shift, Deacon did manage to slip out while Maggie was watching mass on TV, scuttle over to St. James and, before anyone noticed him, disrupt the eleven o'clock service by loudly singing the wrong hymn during the hymn before the sermon. Fortunately, Deacon was fully dressed that morning, actually in a suit and tie, but the disruption made The Reverend T. Randolph

Warren so obviously nonplused that he faltered several times in delivering his otherwise forgettable homily.

But for the most part, Maggie could get Deacon to do what she wanted by telling him that it was what Mrs. Crump wanted him to do. "Mrs. Crump wants you to be nice and do this" she'd say about his eating his vegetables at lunch, or "Mrs. Crump wants you to be nice and not do that," she'd say about his crude belching several times after he had eaten his vegetables. Hearing that, Deacon would shrug, sag a little, and comply.

One afternoon a member of Alice's bridge club commented that Deacon seemed depressed. Alice looked at Maggie, who was sharing desert with the group, and said, "Yes, it is sad. Maggie and I have to struggle sometimes to restrain Deacon from doing things he shouldn't. When we do, he does seem out of sorts for a time, and the only thing that makes it bearable is knowing that what we do is for Deacon's own good." Alice spoke with utter conviction and the members of her bridge club quickly concurred, each adding that she was sure she couldn't manage half so well if she had to face what Alice did. So, under the circumstances, things went along tolerably for Alice and Deacon.

Then one weekend it happened. Weekends were especially difficult for Alice because she was alone in taking care of Deacon, except for Maggie's short Sunday morning shift that allowed Alice to go to church. Occasionally Alice made an arrangement for Maggie to help on a Saturday, but it had to be for a special reason because Maggie spent weekends with her daughter and her family. So usually Alice was completely ready for weekends, having shopped for all of her Deacon's favorite foods and planned all the activities they could do to keep him occupied.

But this particular weekend happened to be Deacon's birthday. Alice had arranged for Maggie to come for an hour late on Saturday morning so she could take care of a few errands in preparation for a party for Deacon to which she'd invited her bridge club and potluck group, most of whom had reluctantly agreed to come. Maggie had made it clear she had to leave promptly at noon in order to attend her grandson's first communion. So when Maggie arrived, Alice had already persuaded Deacon to lie down in bed and rest for a while. Maggie was pleased that everything was calm and that Alice's only instructions were to leave the house open in order to air it out a little.

Alice left feeling confident that Deacon would be fine for the half hour or so she'd be gone. She would go to DeLeone's for fresh flowers and some bayberry candles, to Walker's for party favors and, most important, to Super Mart for the special cake mix they'd been out of earlier in the week. A thirty-minute jaunt, she'd calculated, forty-five at the most.

Everything would have worked out except that each errand took a few minutes longer than she had thought it would. When she left the Super Mart for home, it was already noon. So Alice was driving too fast when she swerved to miss a kid on a bike, hit the curb, blew a tire, and scraped her fender on the pole of a No Parking sign, bending it slightly askew.

By the time she'd gotten everything taken care of with the police, and Triple A had come to fix the tire, over two hours had passed. She'd tried several times to call home but had gotten no answer. None of her neighbors answered their phones either. She was frantic, and when she finally did pull into her garage, she was crying. "Oh please, Lord," she pleaded under her breath as she rushed to the house, "please let everything be all right."

As soon as she opened the door, she shouted, "Deacon! Deacon! Where are you?" She heard only the ominous silence of an empty place and then the ugly roar of a gunshot. She screamed and whirled toward the sound. It seemed to have come from the direction of the church. "Oh, God, nooo!" she moaned, sinking to her knees, hands over her face, imagining bloody disasters in which Deacon was victim or perpetrator.

Then, in a spasm of denial, she whispered, "Maybe it's not him. Oh dear God, don't let it be him." She lurched to her feet and groped her way to the dingy furnace room in the farthest corner of the basement where Deacon kept his shotgun in a little closet near the oil tank. As she reached for the string to pull on the overhead light bulb, she kicked something on the floor. In the swinging light she saw it was an old fondue set amidst discarded Sterno cans and candy bar wrappers. She knelt to examine the fondue pan. It was caked with layers of burned chocolate. The wrappers were from Deacon's favorite candy bars. She'd given them to him and he'd burned them. That was the smell no one could identify. It had wafted up through the heating ducts.

She glanced at Deacon's gun closet and saw that the door was open. "Damnit," she sputtered, pushing herself up, kicking the fondue pan, "damnit, damnit, damnit." She took the stairs two at a time and headed for the church at a trot.

Rounding the corner, she could see through an opening in the trees someone in the high open cupola just where the slate steeple began the sharp ascent to its proudly placed cross. The person was waving what looked like it might have been a shotgun and yelling at someone on the ground below. She realized it was Deacon. Then she saw the crowd and the police cars with flashing lights and the police themselves, dozens of them, lined up, keeping people away. She knew the whole thing was going to be a terrible scandal. What in God's name was Deacon doing up there?

"Son of a bitch, damnit to hell," she gasped, slowing to a walk, surprised by the realization that she was swearing and it felt good. A man at the edge of the crowd turned and started toward her. She recognized Eddie, the church custodian.

"Eddie," she shouted as he approached, "what's going on?"

"It's okay, Miz Crump," Eddie answered, "he ain't shootin' at nobody. It's just that nobody's figured how to get 'im to come down yet."

"What's he doing up there anyway?" she asked, squinting toward Deacon.

Eddie started laughing.

"Eddie, it's nothing to laugh about," she insisted. "He's got a gun. The police are everywhere. Someone will get hurt. Tell me what happened."

Eddie tried to put a sober mask on his face, but it kept slipping away. "Well, Miz Crump, it seems what happened is that the electronic bell thing . . . the, ah . . ."

"Carillon," she interrupted impatiently. "What about it?"

"Yeah, car'lon. Anyhow, it comes on automatic, you know, and the music comes through them speakers up in the tower where Deacon is. Some of the neighbors — you'd know 'em if I could remember their names — tol' the police the car'lon got stuck or something around noon and kept playin' the same thing over and over and over. Nobody was around to turn it off since I was down at the hardware store and then eatin' lunch — over to Ida's Luncheonette, you know Ida's — and the Reverend was off to a funeral, and I don't know where you was. Anyhow, I was just walkin' back when I heard the thing playin' that hymn, you know, 'Amazin' Grace,' only it wasn't playing the whole thing, just this one part over and over again. I knew that wasn't right so I was goin' to check it out soons I got back, but then I heard this shotgun blast and then a couple more. Well, the car'lon stopped all right. What Deacon done was blowed off them speakers we had bolted up there in the cupola." Eddie was laughing again.

"Eddie, stop it. It's not funny," Alice shouted. "It's embarrassing. Dangerous. We've got to get him down." She started toward the crowd.

"Wait, Miz Crump," Eddie implored, "I ain't told you the whole story yet." She stopped and he went on. "Soons I heard that gun, I run to the church and I hear Deacon yellin', 'How sweet the sound, how sweet the sound, how sweet the sound . . . you make me sick, you make me sick, you make me sick.' Then I seen him lean over the edge up there and make like he's throwin' up, makin' awful throw-up sounds, you know, and then yellin' out, 'I'm drownin', we're all drownin' in crap, in a sea of crap, sweet crappy crap, godawful syrup.' Then he raises up that gun and blasts off a couple more shots and starts laughin' like he's havin' hisself a real good time. Anyhow, the neighbors come runnin' from ever which way, and ol' Deacon waves to 'em and yells, 'Hey, I stopped that pukin', sicken' sound, didn't I? Drive you nuts, doesn't it? How sweet the sound, how sweet the sound, my ass. My ass, with the non-deacon bad side showin'.' I ain't got no idea what he meant by that, but then he mooned 'em, Miz Crump. From right up there, he mooned 'em."

"He didn't!" Alice stared at Eddie in disbelief.

Eddie chortled, "Yes ma'am, he did. He's been standin' up there in his underwear firin' off a blast every once in a while, and wavin' at people and laughin' and tellin' the police to get the Mayor down here 'cause he's got a few things to tell him and . . ."

"Why don't they get him down?" Her tone was urgent. "We've got to get him down. It's humiliating."

Eddie looked at her and shook his head. "Well, they been tryin', Miz Crump. Police sent me to get you, but you wasn't home. So the police captain — he's the one in the white shirt with that bullhorn — he's been talkin' to Deacon, but it doesn't do no good." Eddie started to laugh again.

"Damnit, Eddie, stop it. This is damn serious."

Eddie caught the snarl in Alice's words and that, and the swearing, shocked him. "Yes ma'am. What I mean is . . . well, it didn't do no good, that's all."

"Why not? Deacon can be handled easily enough." She was breathing hard.

"Don't seem so, at least in this case," Eddie answered. "You see, the captain there, he got the name of that lady what helps you with Deacon, got it from the Reverend, and he radios his headquarters to call her, which they done. They call back and tell the captain what she said, and then he talks to Deacon on the bullhorn. He keeps sayin', 'Deacon, Miz Crump wants you to be nice and come down now. And . . .'" Eddie hesitated.

"And what?" Alice shouted.

Eddie looked down at his feet and tried to fight back a smile. "And he — Deacon up there — he, ah . . . well he just yelled out plain as sin, 'You tell Miz Crump she's full of crap. To hell with her.' You can ask anyone if he didn't say that, Miz Crump." He turned away giggling.

Alice took a deep breath and growled, "He did, huh? Why that little, spineless, pea-headed jerk. How did he get up there?" She started toward the crowd.

Eddie followed her, still giggling. "He got a ladder from the church basement. He knows where we keep 'em. Don't you do nothin' stupid now, Miz Crump."

As she pushed through the crowd toward the police, Alice noticed the ladder leaning on the shadow side of the tower. Then a voice boomed through the bullhorn, "Deacon, this is Reverend Warren," the voice announced. "In the name of God, please come down. You are bringing disgrace on yourself and your good wife and this church."

Deacon laughed and sang back at the top of his lungs, "'Terrible disgrace, how sour the sound, that saved a wretch like me.' How about that, Reverend? Hey, tell me something. I always wanted to know what that 'T.' in your name stands for."

In spite of herself, Alice smiled. And she realized that Deacon's voice sounded very clear and commanding. She reached the police captain just as Reverend Warren stammered his answer. "Well, it . . . it's just an initial. It doesn't stand for anything. I mean, no name or anything.

Deacon Daniel bellowed, "You mean your parents just gave you an initial as part of your name?"

"It wasn't my parents," Reverend Warren yelled, "the initial was . . . it came later." He meekly handed the bullhorn back to the captain.

An incredulous Deacon shouted back, "You mean you just added the T. yourself? Why? Don't tell me. It was for the high-class sound of it. So no one would even think to call you Randy! Never even think of you as being as earthy as Randy. High class, my ass, Reverend T. Randy, Randy, Randy." The blast of a shotgun filled the air.

Deacon whooped and went on. "And you know what, Reverend T.? You're a deacon, just like me. You know what a deacon is? A fruit wrapped with only the best side showing or maybe a castrated animal. You can look it up, if you want to, Reverend T. old buddy. What d'ya say, shall we give it up? I'll be plain old Danny and you be plain old Randy." Deacon was laughing.

Then he yelled down, "By the way, Reverend T., when you get this thing fixed, why don't you play something besides that sentimental crap once in a while? Broaden out a bit, get religion unstuck. Mix in a little Beethoven or Stevie Wonder every so often. People might love it. At least we could give 'em that, since St. James has been too gutless to do anything else for the city."

Alice started across the churchyard. A cop with a riot helmet on his head caught her and pulled her back. "Where the hell do you think you're going, lady?"

"I'm his wife," she shouted. "Let me go."

He ushered her roughly to the captain. "Here's the guy's wife, sir," he said.

The Captain looked at her wearily, then spoke softly. "Wife? I don't know where you've been or why nobody was watching your husband, and right now, I don't much care." His voice began to rise. "But I want to make one thing clear, lady. Your crazy, goddamn husband is a terrorist, far as I'm concerned. He doesn't get his ass off that tower in about two minutes, we'll shoot it off. You understand? I ain't about to let some fuzzball maniac stay up there shooting a gun until he kills somebody. That clear? Now, you've got two minutes. Here, talk to him." He handed her the bullhorn.

"Just don't shoot him," she demanded, taking the bullhorn. "How does this thing work?"

"Hold it like this. Press this button and talk," he instructed her.

"Okay, but not from here," she insisted, walking quickly out on the churchyard toward the tower.

No one stopped her. "You got two minutes," the Captain called after her.

"Deacon!" Her voice sounded like a roar to her.

"Go to hell, Alice!" Deacon's voice sounded amplified, too. Then he fired the gun in warning.

She kept walking toward the tower. The Captain ordered her to come back. She ignored him. She heard him yell, "Get her, boys!"

She whirled and pointed the bullhorn toward them and yelled, "Stay away from me or you'll regret it. Touch me, I'll sue your asses. And I have witnesses."

The cops retreated. She heard Eddie shout, "You tell 'em, Miz Crump." The crowd cheered.

She turned back toward the tower and started walking. "Go to hell yourself, Daniel Crump." More cheers! She felt excited.

In rapid succession Daniel fired off three or four shots in the air. "Stay away from me, you witch," he screamed at her.

"That's the damn problem," she screamed back. "I've stayed too damn far away from you for too damn long, you . . . you . . . eunuch."

His eyes looked wild and he sputtered, "You . . . you . . . castrating witch. WITCH."

She was at the bottom of the ladder looking up at him. That face she'd known so well suddenly looked like a stranger's to her. She dropped the bullhorn and screamed, "No one gets castrated who doesn't want to be. EUNUCH!"

Glaring down at her, he shouted, "No one's a eunuch who isn't seduced by the syrup. BITCH!"

For a nearly a minute, with the crowd responding with hisses and cheers like a Greek chorus, they hurled insults at each other.

"Bitch!"

"Eunuch!"

"Bitch!"

The excitement of it was contagious between them. Both were surprised by the curious pleasure and power of their feelings.

Finally Alice broke the cadence. "Where have you been, you damned phony? You aren't senile, you bastard!" She began to climb the ladder.

He scoffed, "Who said I was?"

"You acted like it. Doctor Hawkins said so," she replied, pulling herself upward.

"What did Hawkins know? Was he in my head? Hell no!" Daniel countered.

She scowled and climbed higher. "Then, why? Why the hell did you do that to me?"

"Do what to you? What do you mean, where have I been? I've been suffocating under all that damned frosting you spread over everything until I couldn't breathe. Drove me crazy. I've been crazy, that's where I've been."

With each rung she climbed, she shrieked higher, "Don't blame me for your being a damned coward. You always withdrew, walked away. You weren't crazy. You were a coward. Did it ever occur to you that maybe I'd have put on much less frosting if you'd been more cake?" Spit was flying from her mouth.

He howled in derision, "Where was the room for the cake under all that frosting?"

She reached the top of the ladder, threw her leg over the ledge, tearing her skirt open as she did. They stood glaring at each other. Then tears began streaming down Daniel's cheeks. "Oh, no," his voice gravelly but determined. "Noooo. This is too easy, blaming each other. You know what? I think we got sucked into a black hole back there somewhere. A damned black hole called nice or orderly or religious or something. A big black hole nothing could escape from, no not-nice things, no bad feelings, whatever they might be — except passion and anger and conflict and being different were among them. Nothing could escape that black hole. Not playful, not crazy, not light, not even love. That's what happened. It all disappeared in the black hole of "nice." *We* disappeared in the black hole of nice. That's where I've been. Hell, that's where we've all been, near as I can tell."

He wiped his eyes and nose with the back of his hand and leaned on the ledge. "You know what else? I don't know if I can, or if I have enough time, but I'd like to try to escape from that black hole. I was lying there listening to that song, 'Amazing Grace, how sweet the sound . . .' for the damn umpteenth time when all of a sudden it hit me. Why the hell is grace always supposed to be a sweet sound? Hell, why not it's like an explosion, like a Big Bang, right? I couldn't wait to get my damn gun and get over here."

"You're crazy, Deacon. Damn crazy."

"Maybe it's about time."

They stood eyeball to eyeball. The wind up there ruffled her gray hair and smelled fresh. She smiled first. "You look pretty sexy in your underwear, Daniel."

He smiled back. "You look pretty sexy yourself with your dress torn like that."

They started laughing, and the laughter rolled down across the churchyard. She took the gun from him. "How do you work this thing?" she asked. "Oh, never mind." She pulled the trigger. It was an automatic shotgun and recoiled like a bucking horse. Her first shot blew the rainspout off the tower, her second went through the window of the church office, the third took out the windshield of Reverend T.'s Grand Prix, and the fourth blew the top off the Rickenbacker Memorial flagpole, sending both the American and Christian flags crashing to the ground. The gun clicked. It was empty. Alice and Deacon Daniel were in hysterics.

Then the first shots from the police ricocheted off the tower. They ducked. Alice tore the sleeve off her blouse, and they tied it to the shotgun and waved it to the police. They stood and, following instructions over a second bullhorn, threw the gun over, and climbed down the ladder. The crowd cheered.

At the bottom, as the police ran toward them, Deacon said to Alice, "We've got a long way to go."

"So let's go on with it," Alice replied.

That night, after having been fingerprinted, booked for disturbing the peace, released on $500 bail each, and cheered as heroes outside the police station by a large crowd of people who'd seen them on TV, Alice and Deacon Daniel Crump had a birthday party. The invited guests came not sure what to expect and, since everyone was a little tired, left early still not sure what to expect.

But the cake was different. Alice and Daniel had made it together, and it had four layers, full of nuts, raisins and spices with a very thin but lovely chocolate-orange frosting. And on top there was just one candle that, in the dark room, seemed quite bright enough. And, it should be noted, all through the party Daniel remained in his underwear and Alice's dress was still quite revealingly torn.

While they were eating the cake, the sound of Stevie Wonder's song "Isn't She Lovely" suddenly filled the night air. When they went to the door, they saw a Grand Prix with its windshield missing, a speaker mounted precariously on the top, and a sign taped to the side saying, "Eddie and Randy wish the former Deacon a Happy Birthday, and Danny and Alice a good life, for Christ's sake."

It was indeed a Big Bang. No one could be sure what kind of universe would follow or how far it would expand.

Crazed into holy awareness

Come, Lord Jesus,
    confront me as a prophet:
        disturb my indifference,
            expose my practiced phoniness,
                shatter my brittle certainties,
                    deflate my arrogant sophistries,
  and craze me into a holy awareness
    of my common humanity
        and so of my bony, bloody need
            to love mercy,
              do justly,
                  and walk humbly with you
                      — and with myself,
trusting that whatever things it may be too late for,
    prayer is not one of them,
        nor a chance,
           nor change,
              nor passion,
                nor laughter,
    nor starting yet again
        to risk a way to be together,
    nor a wild, far-sighted claim
        that this human stuff of yours
            is stronger still than fail or time,
              graced to share a kingdom
              and spirited for joy.

CHANGES

An accurate reticence

O God, you who wait to be gracious,
　　you who never flaunt yourself,
　　　　what is this tormenting need
　　　　　　to put myself always on display,
　　　　　　to give too much of self away,
　　　　　　to meet every request as if each was a just demand,
　　　　　　　　or Christ never left the crowds
　　　　　　　　　　to withdraw into the wilderness;
　　　　as if there is no essential difference
　　　　　　between others' response and yours,
　　　　　　　　between what I get from them and what I need;
　　　　as if I had no right to anything
　　　　　　that was just mine and yours,
　　　　　　　　a secret that sustains and not a show?
My ambition drains me,
　　this compulsion to prove a truth, a grace
　　　　I do not deeply hold myself,
　　　　　　or let myself be held by.
O God of such unfathomable depths as can alone assure,
　　draw me down to an accurate reticence,
　　　　a waiting resonant with yours,
　　　　　　a self to be chosen, as you do,
　　　　　　　　and plumbed, with you,
　　　　a privacy of faith,
　　　　　　a holding at the core,
　　　　　　　　a human-divine meeting,
　　　　a holy ground
　　　　　　to stand on,
　　　　　　　　and to withstand
　　　　　　　　　　the seduction of a stage,
　　　　　　　　　　　　the temptation of applause.
Calm me to depths I can endure,
　　learn trust, and abide assured
　　　　with abiding,
　　　　　　deeply present,
　　　　　　　　constant,
　　　　　　　　　　sufficient
　　　　　　　　　　　　hidden you.

Something plain as bread

Ingenious One,
    please hear me out,
        so I can hear myself out
            in this chant of complaint,
                this confession of praise.
God knows —
    don't you? —
        I've said all this before,
            prayed it essentially this way,
                perhaps using a few new words I learn,
      but only to recite the same needs,
            quick gratitudes, solicitations,
                propositions, tired guilts,
                    despairs, disguised instructions,
                        timid hopes, embarrassed adorations.

It's as if I'm only what I always was,
    perhaps with a few different ways I mimic,
        but only to make the same responses
            I was conditioned to make before I knew why,
      yet keep making, fall back upon when pushed,
            even though I thought I now knew why not
      after all the sacraments of therapy and church,
            small failures, successes, long-suffering friends.

I get tired of this me, this more-than-one I am,
    of this warring family
        of grandparents, parents,
            brothers, sisters,
                uncles, aunts, cousins,
    all those who, though within your providence,
        yet infused into my bones
            the absolute of right and wrong,
                as if their values were at last
                no less than yours;

of these insidious comparisons
    I was taught to make,
        and make still,
            to my distress and insufficiency;
of the curse, yet blessing,
      of this inheritance I bear,
          my tangled legacy of strengths and weaknesses
          for which I would be grateful
           and want so to forgive.

But I seem stuck in this constant repetition
    of being human
        when I presume I should be more.
        I get stupid with self-pity,
           sunk in discouragement.
             God, it's all so familiar, isn't it?

And yet . . . who knows why, except you,
    something happens,
        more often than I realize I believe,
    something plain as bread,
        clear as wine and lightning,
          taken for granted as salt,
         a bird song,
           a well-worn book,
             lilacs;
    presumed as mother love,
        the laughter of a child,
        a lover's touch,
        Mozart,
           Michelangelo,
           Yeats;

all shudders, shifts, slides,
    bursts like a shaft of light
        into my eyes, my nerve, my heart,
    tingles my fingers,
        raises my neck hair,
            turns my head,
                opens my ears,
                    even now,
    to this awesomely unfamiliar,
        strange familiar life I'm given back again;
    to this enough
        I'm slowly becoming;
    to these critical, small changes
        I've been wounded, weakened,
            willed, and wondered into,
                and cannot truly disregard;
    to all this holy saving going on.

So Ingenious One,
    what I want at last to say
        is thanks
            for the Christly, christening way
                you hear me out,
                    so I can hear myself
                    anew.

Seraphim in disguise

O God,
everywhere present, but nowhere obvious,
      here I am where I always seem to be:
            betwixt cold fronts and crocuses,
                  dreams and disappointments,
                        failures and summons,
                              flaws and gifts,
                                    growing up and growing old;
            betwixt isolation and intimacy,
                  weariness and renewal,
                        despair and hope,
                              confidence and fear,
                                    life and death.
O God,
      you must know how hard it is
            to be in this between
                  where nothing is certain,
                        everything's in flux,
            this relentless churning
                  from something I can't quite grasp
                        to something I can't quite see,
            and it's all up for grabs,
                  and — please God —
                        for grace.
Mercy out of me
      this tumorous sense of fault,
            this dead-weight of doubt
      that I am not two-sparrows' worth,
            and no concern of yours.
Deepen into me
      the liberating assurance
            that I am where you are with me,
      stretched between the kingdom in our midst
            and the slow fullness of its coming.

Muster my courage
    to let go of the clutch of grievances
        that keep rendering me vaguely the same,
    to become vulnerable to surprise — by being one —
        taking some outrageous, specific dare of love.
Strengthen my trust
    that you are in the turbulence
        to intensify my struggles,
    and to render me, as well,
        sociable to joy, subject to your grace.
Keen my awareness
    that uncertainty is my dance with you,
        crises, seraphim in disguise,
    rumpling the air with choice and change,
        tonging the coals of another chance,
            proclaiming betwixt as holy,
                cleansing my soul for gratitude,
                    freeing me, when sent, to go for you,
                  a little less afraid,
                      a little more at ease.

This earthly hitch toward glory

O God,
    who winks quarks and quasars
        and braids Saturn's rings,
    intrigue me out of my shame
        at making mistakes:
                fear of the worst I could do or be
                keeps me from risking my best.

Remind me, again,
    Spinner of galaxies, possibilities,
        and my inquisitive, quivering spirit,
    that what joins me to you
        is less the devout repetition
            of the tried and safely true,
        than the creative dare,
            the imaginative lurch,
        the reworking of the expected
            toward an unexpected new:
                at risk of making errors, yes,
                but faith, and love, and merry, too.

O God, confirm me in my power,
    as I would confirm you in yours,
        for I would claim my power without apology.
    I would be trusting done with this smoldering deference,
        this chafing humility, ingrown virginity,
            quite-too-virtuous denial of strength,
    and just claim this power you gave to me,
        along with all these visions, impulses, hopes, promptings
           that make me laugh, cry, long
                to create the hell out of life —
                    and to heaven with my blunders;
            to make my half-believing self
                somewhat more believing
                and believable.

O God, make me brave, then,
    to use my power to create something original,
        worth the breath and blood and sweat and joy:
                mind over the matter of feared defeats,
                spirit over the specter of tragic error;
    to employ imagination in the squint to see;
    to trust that grace mutates mistakes into surprise,
        like the fall turned into the wondrous history
            of your lover's quarrel with the world and me;
    that what we lost in Eden was our innocence,
        not our power or our freedom or your image in us;
                that your mercy comes as another chance
                I can dare to take.

So would I boldly add my power with your lover's quarrel
    and stand hard for justice,
        reach far for beauty,
            walk long for peace,
                be a worthy adversary of whatever
                demeans and trivializes this humanity;
    thus changing self as well,
        become more fully one of this wondrous, wounded all
            I would go with on this earthly hitch toward glory,
                this graceful twist of history
                you've promised to make with me.

Before I waste away

O God,
    I've been out here too long
        in this wasting competition,
            this shuffle of disguises,
                this diversion of words,
                    this commerce of fear,
    somehow hoping not to be found
        unless I could be found innocent,
            or discovered for accomplishments.

Now I laugh at my damned absurdity,
    laughter, I think,
        your tag of grace,
            my small burst of wisdom,
                and some trust.
    It is, as well, a prayer to change,
        not for the better, but for you,
            and for a self I ache to be
                before I simply waste away.

So I would take something, away from words,
    and listen with it a while:
        not all fear is bad,
            and I would learn from mine.

It's you I've been avoiding,
    and yet seeking, too,
        in all my busy chittering,
            frantic performing,
                frittering tasks,

fearing intimacy I desire
    even in my prayers —
        a towering babble
        telling you less than you know,
        reciting this shopping list
        of impressive petitions
            for self-improvement,
                as if they were the way
                    to you,
    when, if I took the risk of listening,
        I might hear, even now,
        the fearful invitation
        to the fearful novelty
        of shucking the anxiety of unassignments,
            of daring to ask for less,
            and simply taking rest,
                in you.

O God,
    I would no more listen to
        all the self-appointed prophets
            who tell me who not to listen to
    lest I keep missing you,
        missing angels in disguise —
            rejects, bums, clowns, dreamers —
                who make much more than sense;
    and all the more keep missing
        the promptings of my mind,
            the churning of my passions,
    this holy glowing intuition
        that I carry my destination within —
            your image traced upon my soul
                branding me as your own,
                claiming me for
                    the not easy,
                      only rewarding
                        revolution of love.

The downsweep of your wing

O God of storms as well as stillness,
    of questions on which all answers snag,
        of forbidding holiness as well as exciting horizons,
when, as always and as now,
    I don't have enough
        inspiration,
            wisdom,
                imagination,
                    will,
                        or faith
    to do what seems to lay its claim on me,
        or to work the change that seems required,
have mercy on me
    and cover me with grace
        that I may accept,
            however I can,
                these limits of finitude I face,
                    these mortal limits that I am.
Then, grant me to fix upon,
    even with wavering eye
    and wandering mind,
        the glimmer of hope
            without which all is darkness,
that you, less limited than I,
    will find a way to me,
        bestow some gift I cannot name,
        might not choose,
            probably miss as such —
but will persist in its pursuit,
    name me,
        miss not my need
            or my heart —
                though perhaps break both —
and will work the change
    I may not quite believe,
        yet will give me peace enough
            to roll the dice of days again,
                as even now I am about to do.

I take the gamble, O gambling God,
    at the behest of some urge
        I could resist, but won't,
           perhaps to feel —
              ah, that's the pull —
                  the sensual surprise of all my senses
that what lays its too much claim on me
        is really just your claim of me,
the downsweep of your wing,
        your pressing back on pressing me
              through the integrity of this world —
                its stubborn, haunting beauty,
                its resistance to my plans,
                  which breaks my pride,
           its curious loves, perplexing faults,
                the home it is I cannot find —
all of this, and so much more,
        this bearing down of real weight,
           yet tracing, all the while,
              the living weight of me,
ratifying my existence to me,
        strangely rending me more willing
           for the thresh of prayer,
yet, I surmise,
        more strangely still,
           readying me, still quite unknowing,
              for the giddy updraft of grace.

                Is this your prayer
                  for me to hear?

                O God, I'm listening.

SWEET, MOTHER-LOVING JESUS

She was lying in the tub ruminating aloud when the sucking sound of the drain got loud enough to distract her. Enraged at the interruption, she pitched forward, reviling the drain gods, "Just one damn, mother-loving time — is that asking too much?" Her sudden movement created a turbulence of whirlpools and tidal waves, sloshing water over the edge of the tub. As she groped for the wash cloth she'd packed around the drain, she yelled louder, "Sweet, mother-loving Jesus!" She threw the wash cloth against the wall where it sopped up a small patch of paint flakes and flopped to the floor. Freed of that impediment, the water flowed more rapidly down the drain. "Crap," she muttered, and lay back wearily, sending more water splashing from the tub. "Doesn't matter, Norton," she sighed, "nothing matters." She closed her eyes and spit in the air. "No mother-loving, damn thing," she emphasized in the way of someone used to talking to herself or to her long departed husband.

Hannah Holgate's life was reduced to one room and a bath, with a kitchenette on the wall between the hallway door and the bathroom door, in a deteriorating apartment house with which she had a grudging affinity, physically and financially. The lever for operating the drain in the tub had corroded and couldn't be closed tightly, so the water leaked out faster than more water could be added by the balky water heater. A body couldn't soak anything to a comfort or a conclusion.

Resigned to that inevitability, she got out and toweled herself off carefully. She grieved over the spots and folds and creases that must have come slowly upon her body and yet somehow seemed to have arrived with the same shocking suddenness as a late October cold rain quickly turning riotous autumn to somber gray. Hannah appraised herself in the mirror. There was no denying it, but the wonder was that she didn't feel at all as her body looked. Inside, under all the sags, wrinkles, spidery veins, and strangely translucent skin, she felt there was a young woman living as Jonah in the belly of an aged whale.

She assumed a sideways pose. "Hannah Holgate," she whispered to her image, "you ravishing beauty, you turner of heads, you irresistible femme . . ." she turned the other way, "fatale." She dropped the pose and snorted at herself in the mirror, "Right! Fatal's what I got all right. Hannah, if you were to fall over in a forest, would a tree hear? Face it, honey . . . it wouldn't."

She chuckled, held her head back, pulled the skin of her face tightly, and began applying eye shadow while she talked. "Norton, do you suppose my skin's puckering because I've turned bitter? Or maybe I'm just bitter because my skin's puckering." She paused to run lipstick over her lips, purse them together, and then blot them lightly on some toilet paper before concluding: "Either way, it's just too damn bad, isn't it, Norton?"

She shrugged, wrapped the towel around her, flicked off the light switch, and paused in the dark. "The question is, if I'm old, why ain't I wise? The answer is, if I ain't wise, I must not be old." She chuckled, then shrugged. "Or maybe the truth is that all that stuff about the old being wise is a mother-loving myth, Norton. But if that's so, we oughtn't tell anyone or they'll take us off Social Security and Medicare and let us starve, like those people sleeping out there on the sidewalks." She shook her head. "Or maybe I am just crazy, like people say."

She walked into her room, which strained somewhat unsuccessfully to hold the chairs, sofas, end tables, and accumulated bric-a-brac of her sixty-seven years. The twilight softened the shrugging confusion of it and hid places where the water-stained, rambling rose wallpaper had bubbled loose and years of use had scratched and scrunched all the furniture. Around the room she'd hung the familiar pictures that had filled the walls wherever she'd lived for the last fifty years.

Between the pictures, she'd more recently hung, or actually scotch taped, a variety of posters that had caught her fancy, pictures of mountains or meadows of flowers or animals on which were pithy aphorisms, such as, "All we need is an ear to listen, an eye to behold, a heart to feel"; or "A friend comes in when everyone else goes out"; or "Love cultivates, not dominates"; or "None of us is as smart as all of us." She'd liked those posters and simple slogans. They seemed quite religious to her, easily digestible little morsels to feed her soul. Lately though, she'd tired of them as she had of the cheap TV dinners she ate with less and less frequency.

She went to the window, pushed aside a dirty soup bowl on the sill, cranked the window open a crack, leaned on her elbows, and looked out. Far down the street, which ran west to the river, the sky was a smear of indigo and orange running down to crimson, one of those conflagrations that seem to pronounce judgment and give the impression of great fires raging below. It had been raining earlier, and the spring evening felt sodden. The drip of water from the protrusions of the building seemed strangely ominous.

Shivering, Hannah turned from the window, shouting to audibly complete the shiver and to warn whatever furies rode the oncoming night: "Damnit all anyway!" The ensuing silence seemed arrogant. She pressed her hands to her temples. What was it she was supposed to be doing? Was she going out? To a meeting? To a lecture at the Y? Was Norton coming home? For a minute, she couldn't focus. No, it wasn't Norton; he was dead. What was it then? She got things more and more confused these days. Panic nibbled at her edges.

She turned back to the window. She still felt strong physically, and that reassured her. The light from Hahn's, the bargain drug store at the corner, glistened on the wet pavement. She could hear the druggist pulling down the protective grill over the front of the store in preparation for closing. Down from Hahn's was Luc's Convenience Mart, open all night, that was run by a Vietnamese family; then a Deli, a discount appliance store with one display window boarded up, Bryant's cleaners, The Bull's Eye bar, Jack's Pit Barbecued Ribs, McNally's bar, and so on down the block. It was a hip pocket of the city.

Hannah often fantasized about the Hahns and Lucs and Bryants and Jack as she gazed from her window, imagining what their lives were like. But who were they, really? Were they survivors or mutations? In a city, or anywhere, who were the predators, who the prey? Or perhaps a neighborhood is a symbiotic system with changing hosts and parasites. Still, what would happen to these people? Who cared what happened to them? Who had looked out this very same window fifty years ago, or ten years ago, or five? What had they seen? Did it matter? She felt the tears and blinked them back. A man walked his dog through the puddle of drug store light and waited while the dog sniffed and lifted on a hydrant. A bus lurched around the corner and squealed to a stop. Someone got off.

Across the street was the park. In the daytime it was benign; in the night time, malignant. Children played there in the light, demons in the dark. Or so it seemed. She had heard of the terrible things that happened there: drug deals, gang fights, orgies, murders, rapes. There were even stories of people who had gone in there and never been seen again. Even now as she watched, the park appeared to crouch there like some prehistoric beast, its dark heart impenetrable, its tree limbs seeming to twist grotesquely to conceal obscene, nameless terrors, the returned nightmares of child-hood. Sound, light, safety, civilization stopped at the edge of the park, reinforcing her assumption that evil must be silent and invisible. "That park scares me to death, Norton."

She put her fingers to her face and felt again the years layered and grooved there. Something in her knew it wasn't just death that the park embodied to her. It was abandonment, utter loneliness. And fear, fear of the abyss, something unimaginable, bottomless, nameless. If you could name things, they had meaning. If you could name something, it would have a certain order, a tincture of hope. Meaninglessness was what the park threatened. Chaos! Senselessness! That was the word the newspapers often used about things — senseless killings, senseless destruction, senseless violence. Senseless, senseless! That was the terror of the park. It was an abyss! You had to hang on tight to keep from slipping into it.

On the far side of the park, and seeming quite far removed from it, she saw the dark outline of the spire of Christ Church, one of the most well known in the city. She'd been there many times. "It's beautiful, Norton," she sighed softly, "so peaceful — the windows, the music, the prayers. Even from here, you can see it's beautiful. Look!" She cocked her head as if to point, then added plaintively, "But there's that park between." Her brow furrowed. Why was the park there, rubbing its back against her building, its head against that beautiful church? What was the connection? Or was there any? Suddenly she felt an urgency, a confusion. What was she trying to get hold of? She rubbed her eyes. Whatever it was had slipped away. Why did she get so confused sometimes? Why was her brain so balky? "Damn mother-loving everything anyway, Norton!" she fumed.

She padded away from the window, switched on the light, sat on the chrome-plastic stool at the kitchenette counter, and picked up the envelope leaning against the toaster. The address was in familiar handwriting. "Mrs. Hannah Holgate, 15725 Park Drive, Apt. 324." And in the corner that fearful return address: "Susan Holgate, Central State Hospital . . ." It had come three days ago. She pulled out the letter, unfolded it carefully, and read yet again:

Dear Mother,

I'm in the hospital again. To say the least, I'm discouraged. And scared. Everything seems so damned hard, so impossible. Three breakdowns in four years. Guinness Book of Records, right? I keep telling myself I'm really making progress, getting better, that this is a learning experience. But I'm sick of plastic optimism.

You always told me life was a continuous learning experience, a building process, each change bringing us a bit closer to fulfillment. Be positive, you said. Everything will work out. I hate to tell you, Mom, but that's a lot of bull. My life keeps falling apart. So tell me why. What's the truth?

I ask Chaplain Charlie here, and all he can say is that I have to trust God's love, that all this is for my good and I have to make it work for me. Can you believe that? What in Christ's holy name is that supposed to mean? I keep asking C. C., and he just keeps smiling and says we'll keep working on my problems and some day I'll understand. When he said that this morning, I screamed at him, "We? We'll keep working? How the hell are you working on it? You going to sleep with me tonight? Maybe that would help." Then I laughed like a fiend. He just patted my arm and left, smiling. Condescending bastard!

Christ, I'd like to crack his sanctimonious pose. Hell of it is, he probably doesn't even know it's a pose! Every morning at 8 or so, C.C. wheels in in his nice little Honda and does his nice little job and around 5:00 he heads back to his nice little house and nice little family he's always talking about and reads his nice little books. And he's the expert! Me? I lie on my cot and listen to the babble of this damn place and get crazier. It's unbelievable.

Well, I wish I could send some good news to you. I guess I'll just have to try again to get my life back together. But I feel panicky. I feel like I've just got to get out of here, one way or another.

Think of me, Mom.

Susan.

Hannah felt defeated. "One way or another," she echoed. Once, Susan had overdosed on sleeping pills and almost died. "Is that what she means, Norton?" she shouted over her shoulder before dropping the letter on the counter. She put her head down. "O dear God," she whispered, "dear God . . ." What was it she wanted to say? "Damn you!" she said through clenched teeth. Yes, that was it. "Damn you, help her! Help her! Help me!"

She stood and paced, thinking about the phone call she'd gotten late that afternoon from Doctor Somebody or other. "I have a call for Hannah Holgate from Doctor Whoever-it-was," the operator said. "Is this Hannah Holgate?"

Then the doctor's voice came on, sounding so detached and professional, saying things she couldn't quite grasp through her slippery fear: "We thought you should know . . . daughter . . . unauthorized departure yesterday . . . notified the authorities . . . quite sick . . . unpredictable behavior . . . be sure to let us know."

It wasn't until he'd hung up that her question focused. She yelled into the dead phone: "Let you know what? What? I thought you were supposed to know!" That's when she'd run the water for her bath. Now she wondered why. What was it she thought she'd do? What was she supposed to do?

"Get dressed, Hannah," she said so loudly it startled her. "Yes, get dressed, it'll come to you." She lurched toward the closet and collided with a chair. The towel dropped off. Tears welled up again. She sank into the offending chair. "Sweet, mother-loving Jesus, help me. Please."

"What Susan says *is* true, isn't it Norton?" she said, beginning to cry. She had believed that life was about continuous progress toward better things, that a positive attitude helped solve temporary setbacks, that a better world was possible because people were basically good. She'd held onto that even when Norton had died after nine hellish months of constant care following a stroke and Susan had been in mental hospitals a couple of times. And God was sort of . . . well, love. Kind of a cross between a Disney Prince Charming and a Clint Eastwood type dealing with the bad guys. Yes, that actually just about described it. She smiled quaveringly at the image. Or maybe these days, judging from what she picked up in the news, God was more a cross between Snow White and Gloria Steinem.

Suddenly the unexamined triviality of it overwhelmed her, and she began to sob. "Oh God, I love Susan. What can I do?" What Susan said seemed true, that believing everything would work out was a lot of bull. The world really wasn't any better after all these years. She'd voted once for Norman Thomas, had been for the New Deal, the Fair Deal, all those deals, advocated population control, marched for civil rights and against wars — and if anything, the world had just as many problems as before that were, if anything, more dangerous ones. So who was the enemy? Where was the enemy?

"I'm not going to think about it anymore, Norton," she insisted. "I have to get dressed and go now." She walked naked to her tiny closet, quickly chose from her meager collection and got dressed quickly: hose with only one run in each, scuffed patent-leather shoes with the low heels, red dress, rust jacket. The only neck scarf she could find was turquoise. She tied it in place.

Then on an impulse, she got down on her hands and knees and reached unsuccessfully toward the back of the closet. A stuffed chair blocked the door from opening fully. She pushed the chair with her legs. The door just cleared. She reached in and got out an inlaid jewelry box. She opened it and took out a huge medallion. Her grandmother had given it to her mother, who had given it to her. Her mother had died politely disappointed in her for some unspoken reason she had never understood but still had tried to rectify, even after her mother's death.

But Hannah had never worn the medallion. For one thing, it was so large and heavy. It had a wide, sculpted metal frame encircling an enameled replica of Michelangelo's earthy, lusty painting of the Holy Family. It must have weighed at least a pound, counting the heavy chain. She slipped it over her head and stood. It swung awkwardly, giving her a slight off-balance feeling as she walked. She paused, feeling dizzy. "Never mind, Norton," she declared with a wave of her hand, "it's time."

She left the apartment house uncertain where she was going or what she was looking for. She started walking. The dizziness increased, things began to blur. She walked faster. Sounds echoed in her head: Susan's colicky cry when she was a baby; the rattle of Norton's breathing after his stroke; the bath water gurgling down the leaky drain; that distant voice on the phone: "unauthorized departure . . . unpredictable behavior." She was sure the incessant, distracting ringing in her ears came from the park.

The ringing turned louder, the ringing of a cash register. She heard the buzzing of talk, glass clanking, dim music from somewhere; a blue and red neon sign was floating through smoke. She realized she was in a bar. A hand was stroking her, here, there. The face's breath was sour. Its lips were moving. She tilted her head trying to focus. The lips were saying, "Come on, babe. Drink up and we'll just get on out of here."

She shook her head trying to clear it. "Who are you?" she pleaded.

"Hey," the face leered at her, seeming to speak from under water, "that don't make no difference, now does it? Just say I'm a buyer, you're a seller." The hands began moving over her again.

She felt sick. How did she get here? "Wait," she stammered, "I've got to . . . to . . . get some air."

"Sure thing, baby," face nodded knowingly, "me, too. Come on, let's get some . . . air." The face winked, floated up; the hand took her arm.

"Oh, please, no," she whispered, then more loudly, "Please. I'm no . . . no seller." The grip tightened on her arm, a hand fondled her. "Please don't," she shouted, "Sweet, mother-loving Jesus. Stop it!"

She tried to push the hand away. Jesus? She struggled to remember . . . prostitutes . . . could she be one? . . . they used the park to . . . to do business. She did know that, but . . . Jesus? . . .

Mary Magdalene his friend because . . . because prostitutes . . . prostitutes . . . what? What?" She began to cry. "Because he . . . they . . . prostitutes know something about . . . about the park. Yes, what they knew was . . . was . . .

The hand was under her skirt, fumbling at her garter belt. She swung wildly, hitting the face. "Stop it," she shouted struggling to her feet. "Leave me alone." She started to move away.

The hand grabbed at her dress. "Hold on, bitch," the face growled. The fabric tore.

She stumbled, caught herself. "Lemme go," she screamed.

"Damn whore," the face bellowed, "who'd'ya think ya are, hittin' me?" The hand shoved her hard.

She fell, exposed. She tried to cover herself, to get up, but she slipped down again. There was whistling, jeering, laughing all around her. She rolled to her hands and knees, pushed herself up, stumbled toward the Exit sign shining over the door. Hands pinched, pawed her.

Then she was outside running, crying. "Help me! Sweet, mother-loving Jesus, help me," she sobbed, dodging cars, people, gasping for air, stopping to lean against a wall. "Norton? Norton?" she called, "Where am I supposed to be? Norton?" She bit her knuckle to stifle a scream when she recognized the wall as the wall around the park. Sheet lightning flickered across the sky.

Frantically, she ran back across the street. Cars honked at her. She reached the other side, slowed to catch her breath. At the corner, a street preacher was beseeching pedestrians. Two or three had stopped in disbelief, others walked on laughing and shaking their heads. She paused, mid-sidewalk, gaping. The preacher was wearing only boxer shorts and sneakers, catcher's shin-guards and chest-protector, and a bicycle helmet. She started to chuckle. He looked like a kid at play but was yelling and carrying on like someone demented. On one arm he had fastened a metal garbage lid, and in the other hand he waved a bayonet.

"Go on, laugh," he shouted, "I don't mind being a fool for Christ. But you," he pointed at them with his bayonet, "the Bible says you will be damned fools if you don't take for yourselves the whole armor of God, the breastplate of righteousness, the helmet of salvation" — with each reference he touched the articles on his body with his bayonet — "the shield of faith, the sword of the Spirit" — holding his bayonet aloft — "otherwise, St. Paul tells us, otherwise the powers of darkness and wickedness will be too strong for you" — emphasizing the words with the stage whisper and knowing wink of an informer — "the fiery darts of the devil will be too much to quench." As if in the mockery of a comic opera, sheet lightning flashed, and a few drops of rain began to fall.

Advancing toward him, Hannah screeched, "What in the name of sweet, mother-loving Jesus are you talking about, you maniac?"

The sight of her coming at him startled him. "I'm not a maniac," he protested, "I'm an ambassador for Christ." The words seem to restore his zeal. He began to roar, "You are the maniac if you do not listen. I'm talking about principalities and powers, the hosts of wick-ed-ness!" He lifted and shook his arms in punctuation.

She arrived in front of him, grabbed each side of his chest protector, and pulled him toward her, speaking in an intense rumble, "What are these hosts? Where are they? Have you ever seen them? Where are they? Where?"

She began to cry and shake him. The preacher tried to hold her off without dropping his shield. They both tripped over the curb and fell in a tangled heap. She wrestled free. Faces in the crowd that had gathered were blurred, laughing. She sat, screaming at them, crying, "Please, tell me where I'm supposed to be? Where? I don't know . . . don't know what I was doing back there, in that bar." She pointed wildly. "And Susan . . . Susan's . . . unauthorized but . . . where? Where? Tell me if you know!" No one answered. The rain shower suddenly came harder.

She struggled to her feet, wiping her tears, her leaking nose, on the back of her hands. "And y-y-you," she wheeled suddenly, pointing at the stunned preacher and shuddering to the end of her crying, "you d-d-don't really know a d-d-damn, a mu-mu-mother-lah-lah-loving th-thing. You just t-t-talk. And, and, and strut around like a, a mu-mu-monkey and pass the hat to bu-buy booze. You're no am-ambassador, for G-God's sake. You're just a se-seller, hoping for bu-buyers, like them," her arm swept toward the crowd. "It's all, it's all . . . prostitution."

Suddenly she knew where she had to go. She turned, lurched back across the street toward the park. One heel had broken off. She kicked off both shoes and left them in the street. The preacher shouted after her, "Hey, who do you think you are?" She didn't pause. She'd heard that question before. "Hey, lady, wait a minute. God is not mocked. Come back!"

She was in the shadows at the edge of the park before she stopped to catch her breath. The rain shower had ended, but over her gasping she could hear the rain still dripping off the trees. An occasional sheet of lightning rippled the sky. Spring smells of decay and fecundity mixed in the heavy air. She'd entered the park on the sidewalk by one of the streets that taxis and cars used to cut across town. Now she left the street on a pedestrian path and leaned against a tree. She felt suddenly and overwhelmingly alone, entirely alone, beyond the help of protection of law and order, of words or reason, of kinship or friendship, even of her Eastwood-Steinem God. She'd decided on this course, this baiting of the beast, as a purging, a daring, a searching, but she was as frightened as she was determined. "What is it I'm looking for, Norton?" she whispered, "sweet, mother-loving Jesus, tell me."

She took a deep breath and listened. Nothing. But it was even less than nothing. It was the nothing she'd heard on the telephone when it rang and there was no reply to her hello, no sound, and she'd listened for a moment to the silent listener, and then checked the locks on all the doors. She shivered and began to walk. She heard a sound behind her and picked up her pace, not looking back. Lightning skittered across the sky. In the distance she thought she saw someone walking toward her on the path.

She squinted intently at the small probe of light from the one still-working lamp along the pathway twenty or thirty yards ahead. At the edge of the light someone was walking. A familiar, pigeon-toed sway. Tall. A skirt. In the mist and dim light she couldn't tell. Was it really someone or was it just her imagination?

She heard the noise behind her again. She heard herself whimpering, "Oh sweet, mother-loving Jesus. Please!" It was so dark, so threatening. She was jogging now, as fast as she could. She tried to think. It was urgent. The point . . . about Jesus and . . . and prostitutes and . . . the park? What was it? What?

"Norton," she shouted, as if he'd help her think of it. All she heard in response was someone behind her running, yelling something. Ahead she saw sudden movement in the shadows, heard scuffling, a muffled cry. She had seen somebody.

"Be sure to let us know," the voice had said.

"Let you know what?" she screamed now into the darkness. Then she stopped. She knew.

"Susan?" she called, as a mother calls a child home from play, expecting an answer. It was ominously quiet. She ran toward where she'd seen the scuffling. "Susan! Susan!" she shouted. An arc of lightning etched things in sharp relief. In that second she spotted bushes moving off to the side. Then she heard the sound of struggle. She tore toward the sound, wet branches slapping at her. She pushed through to an open space. Someone grabbed her. "Help!" she screamed, "Sweet . . ."

A hand covered her mouth. "Shut the hell up, whore. You know you askin' for it, comin' in the park alone like this. So you gonna get it. Probably even like it, tell the truth. Know I'm gonna." The hand ripped at her dress, tearing it half open.

She bit and kicked at the same time. A fist hit her hard on the ear. She fell and rolled quickly to her knees. Almost reflexively she pulled the medallion over her head and gripped the chain tightly in her fist. Lightning flashed once, twice. In that instant she saw a man in front of her, unzipping his pants. Beyond him in the clearing she could see Susan's face past the shoulder of another half-naked man kneeling over her, pinning her against the base of a tree with a knife against her throat.

"Susan," she shouted, "Susan."

As the darkness returned to swallow everything, she heard the choked question, "Mom?"

"It's me, Susan," she shouted, trying to sound reassuring. Then she squeezed her eyes shut in terror and gasped, "Sweet, mother-loving Jesus, have mercy." She opened her eyes. They adjusted quickly to the darkness. "Don't hurt her," she pleaded. "Let her go, I'll stay. I'll do anything."

"Well, ain't this somethin', Lefty? " drooled the man in front of her. "Extra thrill, them being mother and daughter, ain't it?" Holding up his pants with one hand, the man cackled and stepped toward her.

"Rape," she screamed, "Help! Rape!" She was on her feet, swinging the medallion. It hit the man's head with a thud. He staggered, slipped down.

She kept swinging and screaming. Then she became aware of another voice bellowing, "The Lord of hosts, the Lord of hosts." She recognized the street preacher. She saw him kick at the man holding Susan. The man fell away, kicked back, and the preacher fell. They began wrestling awkwardly in the mud. Susan staggered to her feet, pulling her skirt down.

"Run, Susan, run!" she screamed. She saw the man plunge his knife into the preacher. "Run," she screamed again, taking a step toward Susan.

But the man who'd stabbed the preacher jumped up and grabbed Susan. As they struggled, the preacher tried to grab the man's legs. By the time Hannah saw the man she'd hit with her medallion lurch to his feet beside her, it was too late. His punch knocked her off her feet.

She landed in a twisted, awkward position, her mouth full of blood and mud. She pushed herself to a sitting position and started swinging her weapon. It was hitting something. There was a groan. She climbed to her feet, slipping uncertainly. Someone kicked her in the stomach. As she fell, she swung her medallion one last time, as if she was splitting a log with an ax. Then she was on her hand and knees, retching. Then as the darkness opened under her, she thought, "It can't hurt me now. I can still see. There's enough light."

Then she was floating. She was a little girl on a swing, pushed higher and higher, invited to jump. She did. The sun was bright in her eyes. Beautiful birds sang around her, but their song was strangely raucous. Everything felt warm and soft. She landed in a cloud of flowers, all different colors. Bees were buzzing, sniffing, talking. She could understand them.

"Careful," they said. And "easy." And "broken." And "lucky . . . alive."

She opened her eyes. Flashing lights seemed to be everywhere. She was strapped to something soft. There was a cool hand on her forehead. Then a pinpoint of light flashed in one eye, then the other. A man's voice assured her, "You're going to be okay. Just take it easy. We're going to the hospital in a minute. You'll be okay."

How did they know? "Norton?" she croaked, "how did . . ." She coughed up mucous and blood.

"Take it easy." The voice became a man with a mustache leaning over her, wiping her lips.

Another voice hovering at the edge of her vision asked, "Norton's the guy in the shorts and chest protector?"

She tried to answer but it was too complicated. She nodded. The pain was sharp and she winced.

The voice went on. "Easy. Norton's seriously hurt, but his chest protector may have saved his life. Knife wound didn't reach his heart. He managed to stagger out to the street and a squad car happened to spot him. Otherwise . . ."

The voice trailed off. She followed the sound of it to a woman standing at her shoulder, wearing a yellow baseball cap, holding a bag with a tube running down to her. She could feel the needle in her arm.

Another voice from somewhere: "Ground bein' slippery didn't hurt nothin' either. Gave the broads better odds 'gainst those punks."

Another voice: "Did ya' see th' medics hadda pry that damn medal outta her hand? Cut th' scum up good with it. Probably hav'ta go to emergency afta we book 'em."

She turned her eyes back to the mustache face. "Susan?" she whispered through puffed lips.

"The other woman?" mustache man asked gently.

She nodded, holding her breath, suddenly teary.

"She said she's your daughter." The mustache man smiled.

Hannah let out her breath at the smile. "Yes," her voice was hoarse, her smile weak in return.

"She's been pretty badly hurt, but I think she's going to be okay," the mustache man assured her. "They're with her now. You're both lucky."

"Sweet . . ." she started to whisper, but then she felt herself being lifted, rolled into place. She realized it was an ambulance. The man and woman with the yellow cap were there, too. Someone else was on the other side of the small enclosure. It was very bright. A door closed. They were moving. A siren sounded far away.

A strange man in a green pajama-type shirt with dark stains on it bent over her and showed her the medallion. There was blood on it. "I hear this is yours," he said, "Maybe you'd feel better if you held it." He put it in her hand.

She nodded and closed her fingers around it. She wanted to ask how he knew it was hers, but the man went right on.

"The police may want it back sometime. I can tell you it did a lot of damage," he confided, winking approvingly.

She tried to clear her throat. She whispered, her eyes filling with tears, "Damage?" What was it? What wasn't it? She felt very confused.

"Yes. I was the first to check the guys who assaulted you," green shirt man nodded, wrapping something on her arm, pumping it tight. "The scalp of one was split open. You must have done that. The calf muscle of the other was badly cut. I'm not sure how you managed that."

"Preacher," she croaked, but the green shirt man was paying attention to something else.

"But that medal probably saved your life," he concluded, unwrapping the thing on her arm, patting her easily on her shoulder. He said something to the mustache man and turned back to the other side of the ambulance.

Assuring her that he'd try not to hurt her, the mustache man inserted a new needle near where the other had been and taped it in place.

Slowly, Hannah's eyes followed the green shirt to the other side. She'd been wanting to look over there since they'd loaded her into the ambulance, but she hadn't quite been able to bring herself to it. She was afraid of what she might see. Yet she hoped.

Her eyes met Susan's staring back, unblinking. Her first thought was that Susan was dead. Then she realized the eyes were glazed, as a child's, with utter weariness and pain, yet were quite alive, focusing on her across the narrow aisle. Her daughter's hair was matted with blood, her check swollen and badly scraped, blood caked at the corner of her mouth. But her eyes were fully open.

"Susan," she rasped. She strained to remember what it was she wanted to say, to find the words. "I . . . I don't know why your life keeps . . . why it keeps falling apart. I just don't . . . know. Forgive me, honey."

Tears filled Susan's eyes, pooled at the bridge of her nose, overflowed. Her words came slowly, weighted by pain, soft with wonder, "Mom . . . it's . . . okay . . . you were . . . there . . . for me . . . a tiger . . ."

"You for me, too," Hannah whispered. "Thing is . . . I'm not sure why . . . why it came together like that, either. It's . . . strange, honey." She was surprised at saying that, but having said them, the words made sense. Maybe that was what she'd been trying to get hold of about Mary Magdalene. But it was too hard to think about now.

"Yeah . . ." Susan gasped, a small smile fluttering through her pain. Before she could go on, she coughed.

"You better take it easy," the mustache man cautioned.

The green shirt man, checking Susan's pulse, glanced up and said, "Might be more important they talk," he said.

Susan struggled to get the words out. "Yeah . . . strange . . ." She grimaced. "God . . . maybe?"

Hannah looked in Susan's eyes, waiting, wondering. "Could be," she whispered, "sweet, mother-loving Jesus . . . it could definitely be . . . yes."

Susan's eyes closed. Hannah felt frightened, but the green shirt man didn't change expression. He kept holding Susan's hand. The mustache man leaned up and wiped off Hannah's brow.

"Susan?" she called hoarsely. "Susan."

Slowly Susan opened her eyes, and her effort to smile succeeded in only one corner of her mouth. Her eyes closed, then opened again.

"You can't . . . give up, honey" Hannah insisted, her voice cracking. "This time I'll . . . I'll be with you. Hear?"

Ever so slightly, Susan nodded her head.

Hannah opened her hand and turned her medallion so Susan could see it. With great effort Susan's eyes went to the medallion, then questioningly back to her mother's face.

"Goes back . . . to your great-grandmother," Hannah said softly, as if beginning bedtime story. "Now . . . it's yours."

She lifted it toward Susan, but it was too heavy and slipped from her fingers. Only the chain around her thumb saved it from falling. She looked at the mustache man. "Please," she whispered.

The mustache man took the medallion and gently put it in Susan's hand. Susan closed her fingers to hold it, then closed her eyes.

Weariness and a kind of peace overtook Hannah. She closed her eyes too, watched the little galaxies of light whirl in that darkness, and asked almost inaudibly, "Does where we're going have a tub with a drain that doesn't leak?"

No once and for all

O Holy One,
    I am distressed at how slowly,
        if at all, I am being made new.
    How long must I put up with me,
        or how long must you?
    I wonder into sighing
        and grope for a longer view.

O Eternal One,
    free me of this double curse
    of always wondering how I'm doing
    while I'm doing all things else,
        as if the how were your measure,
        not the measures that I've learned
            from a thousand other teachers
            I'm more afraid to disappoint
            than myself . . . or you.

When everything seems to change but me,
    ease my peevish self-punishments
    that proudly lack all sense of you,
    and throw around me the mantle of your mercy,
        that I may be more honest and more gentle
        with my deluded, grasping self
            when I, a simply beloved creature,
            fall short of the godly ideals
            to which, like the first Adam, I aspire.

Then soften me into your patience
      as again, and yet again, and always one more time,
      I must go on to wrestle these old demons of mine —
      rage and fear and envy, dis-ease and self-deception —
          which I never really overcome once and for all;
          and, as a blessing, a disjointing of my demands,
              remind me there is no once and for all
              in this earthly pilgrimage I'm on,
              that I may limp to a more graceful rhythm.

Scale my eyes to see afresh,
      gladden my spirit to embrace
      the small yet critical, slow yet cumulative changes
      I have nurtured, and been renewed by, over my seasons,
          and open my head to understand, my heart to trust
          that my willingness to struggle makes me wondrous,
              my flailing reach toward you is yet your gift to me,
              and the one thing I can brave to do better than anyone
              is to keep seeking, faithfully, my truest self with you.

MORTALITY

Daring the embarrassments

Holy Spirit,
        I am weary of the scurry
                of many words and much doing,
        worn thin by the scour
                of time's relentless passing,
        warped by claims and expectations
                I take on but cannot meet,
                        lay out but cannot collect.
Holy Spirit,
        this mortal thus unmade
                turns now to you to be remade.
Shush me to a stillness
        in which I can abide,
                unthreatened, for a time,
and let the wave of your grace
        roll, break, spread
                on the shore of my soul,
until there is healing in me,
        healing through me;
until I catch the eternal note
        on the far side of silence,
                signaling me to live
                        by daring the embarrassments
                                of reworking what's reworkable
                                        with trust, and love, and mercy,
until some rusted, twisted crux of me
        unlocks, releases, opens like a tomb,
                responding to my knock and your command —
                        as I sense happening even now —

and I slip at last into accurate place,
    into the strangely familiar
        wilderness landscape of my soul,
          my exodus to freedom
              out of fear to courage,
              out of despair to hope,
              out of self-pity to creativity,
out of faithless resistance to mortality —
    this fearful, distracting kicking
        at shadows lapping at my feet —
to shifting my eyes from downward glance
    toward stars outshining darkest night,
    streams within the wilderness,
        wondrous pilgrims on the way,
      the promised land,
          the cruciform bridge,
        and you.

Fall in the soul

You have made for everything a season
    and yet, O God,
        when leaves turn and flowers fade
I'm reminded again
      it's always autumn in the soul,
or perhaps "fall"
      is the better term,
        that end of innocence,
          that primal whispered warning
            coming with self-consciousness —
      that second consciousness
        of fleeting time,
          quite finite talent.

O God, it's always fall in my soul;
    first the burst of glorious color,
      then paring winds of discontent,
        the rains of guilt and dread,
and, as in autumn on beloved earth,
    I turn up the collar of my coat,
      my well-worn, half-belief,
        and this thin, groping prayer,
    against the sunset chill,
      the passing, passing, passing
        of all I long for not to pass.

Oh, the longing, Lord,
    this longing that remains,
      this longing that I am.
        Will nothing quiet it
          in this beautiful, terrible world?

There's this strange nostalgia,
    this something I can't quite remember,
      muffled as I am
        in things I do not need,
    this fabled and flawed searching
      with a candle
        for the sun.

What is it I cannot live without?
    What is it I cannot die without?
      What, but you?

Come, Lord, into the fall of me.
    I pray for grace to deal with
      what finally cannot be dealt with,
        and so must be faced in every season
          I am made for, and yet made in,
            glorious burst
            and wind, rain, chill —
              the shadows in my heart,
              the ambiguity of my works,
              the struggles of my conscience,
              the ambivalence of my desires,
              the duplicities of my choices,
              the limits of my perceptions,
              the vacillations of my will,
              the finitude of my powers,
           and always the crinkling of the leaves,
              the creep of spidery wrinkles,
              the setting of the sun;
    yet, in the longing that I am
      is a promised, tender-mercied, graceful spring
        past every fall.

O God, grant me the grateful, sore compassion
      to take nothing for granted
            in this not-to-be-taken-for-granted time,
                  fragile as I'm learning that I am,
                        and much less in control,
                  vulnerable to any-moment, why-not-me
                        crashes, viruses, clots, lumps, losses . . .
                              and great leaps of originality;
      to take nothing any-season-ever for granted:
            neither beauty nor ugliness,
                  friends nor enemies,
            joy nor pain,
                  music nor moans,
            laughter nor tears,
                  life nor death,
            nor love,
                  nor love,
                        nor love,
            nor this urgent longing that I am;
      for it is you I long for
            in all this longing,
      you I seek the more
            in praying for a sore compassion,
      you I cannot live
            or die without,
      you who, I pray, indwell
            in this fall of me
                  to deal with what
                        cannot be dealt with,
                              save with you.
O God, breathe life
      and fire and faith
            into this crumbling clay of me,
      for by the mystery of you,
            the cross, the empty tomb,
      is all, can all become,
            even autumn and this fall,
                  grace upon grace upon grace,
                        and I an act of praise.

Kept by enthusiasms

O God,
    how awesome
        is this spirit-driven creation,
            this sensuous connection
                of my body with the earth
                    and other creatures like myself —
                        and yet not quite;
    so I would begin
        by some mysterious plan
            to learn a little
                what it means
                    to be a lover,
                    and a beloved —
                              the cross also being
                              a spirit-driven,
                              bodily thing.

So I am grateful
    for this body,
        my mortal definition in time and space
    for the joys it knows,
        amidst the pains,
and I accept, reluctantly,
    the wear of time on it
        and its oh-so-reluctant betrayal of me,
            growing slower on the inclines.

So I pray to you,
    who pronounced creation good,
        to pour out your spirit on me
    that I may keep, and be kept by,
        my enthusiasms —
            enthusiasm meaning,
                I once learned,
            being taken from behind
                by god, overwhelmed,
                    wrestled down, up, on.

So take me, God,
    I'm slower now,
        easier to catch,
           and needy.
Renew me in the face of the forces of cynicism
    and too much religiosity
        that would drain me of life's juices,
that even now I may grasp
    that more things are possible for me,
        yea probable,
           than the councils of security
              or the cautions of age
                would bid me believe, or try,
and having grasped,
    be grasped by them.

Take me, God,
    frontwise, sideways, from behind,
        that I may dare to stand for my convictions,
           remove a small plug to let justice' waters roll,
        speak boldly for my visions and of mercy, too,
           though others scoff,
        and live as Christ lived,
           daring others to love or reject me
              for who I am
           rather than pandering to be liked, accepted
              for what I am not
                but pretend to be.

Take me, God,
    anyway you will,
        keeping me young in your spirit,
        and aware of what young truly is:
           eager, curious, dauntless,
              willing to explore, to struggle,
           to be foolish as the world goes,
              foolish, caring, trusting, open,

and brave,
> mortality not being for cowards
> and courage being contagious
>> (unless the inoculation of security
>> has taken overly)
> since I caught a small dose from others,
>> and one or two who follow
>> might catch a bit of it from me.

Take me, God,
> that while yet in this body,
>> this sensuous connection
>>> with the earth
>>>> and other creatures,
> I may learn the more
>> to be a lover,
>>> and a beloved,
>> to do love's labor
>>> stronger than time —

the cross being
a bodily thing
though spirit-driven;

and learn as well
> to stretch toward resurrection,
>> as I did toward birth,
> by pushing trustingly against
>> the limitations.

Take me, God,
> and grant me grace
>> to watch for you
>>> in winter's skies as well as spring's,
>>> in empty places as well as full,
>>> in grandmothers' hands as well as children's,
> and in mystery perhaps to see
>> you in the eye
>>> of this one watching,
>>>> enthusiastically.

Unearthly longings

O God of history,
        you created me
                as you created each of this human clan,
        a creature of time and space
                which I cannot escape,
        but with intimations of transcendence
                which I cannot achieve,
        and I am awash with longing
                as of moon and sun and starlight.

Come now
        to confirm these terrible,
                wonderful, unearthly longings
                        as the light of you in me.

O God of the human generations,
        all that struggled from ice age until now,
                looking for everything on earth,
                        and yet for more,
        and so God of me,
                and of all my times
                        of sighs and aches, glories, triumphs,
                                defeats, and interminable in-betweens,
                        of all the painful work and painful waiting,
                                the wondrous having and the awful losing;
        move with me now in my season of struggle,
                as in other seasons your spirit moved
                        to give prophecies to children,
                                visions to the young,
                                        dreams to old men and women,
                        and to all that struggled from ice age until now,
                                looking for everything on earth,
                                        and yet for more —
                                                as have I in my short life,
                                                        and do the more intently now.

O God,
  this time and space I cannot escape,
      this mortality I'm stuck in
          constrains in many relentless ways:
              in fading inspiration,
                  waning energy,
                      shortening expectations,
                          troubled sleep,
      leaving me with the caution of experience,
          questions without answers,
              yet worthy duties to be done,
          and fidelity the only way past
              the circuitries of intellect,
                  the shifting sands of knowledge.

O God,
  I want to scream this prayer,
      curse out my frustration,
  for my passion has not wrinkled away,
      nor has this light of you,
          this unearthly, terrible,
              seething longing,
                  been doused;
  and so, you surely know,
      my screams, my curses,
          like the melody of songs,
              would be praises stripped of nice words.

O God,
  move with me now,
      abide with me in my urgenting need
          when the petals of spring wither,
          when summer ends before what's planned,
          when autumn sends chill winds to scout,

and I am caught, cold sweat found out,
　　　hanging on for dear life
　　　　　to the whipping end of it;
　　　so much started,
　　　　　so little done,
　　　so many promises made,
　　　　　so few delivered on,
　　　so many loves unspoken,
　　　　　so many wrongs ignored,
　　　so much gratitude unspoken,
　　　　　so much mercy long withheld,
and now I'm scrunched up behind the tasks,
　　　with time shriveling up ahead.

O God,
　　　grant me strength to bear these burdens
　　　　　but first,
　　　　　　　spiritual sight to glimpse the more
　　　　　　　you set my heart on from the start;
　　　grant me energy for my duties,
　　　an ingenious way through some dead ends,
　　　　　but first,
　　　　　　　spiritual sight to glimpse the more
　　　　　　　you set my heart on from the start.

O God,
　　　help me to separate the essential from the trivial
　　　　　in these however many remaining days
　　　　　　　I would shape and which shape me,
　　　that in the separating
　　　　　I may glimpse the more,
　　　　　　　the kingdom
　　　　　　　you set my heart on from the start.

O God,
  I come driven to you
    by what I cannot escape
      and what I cannot achieve,
    by what I am,
      yet what I'm not,
 wanting passionately now to live for joy,
    not with regret or for some gain;
to gladly be this creature you created,
   to accept my years,
     my mortal limits,
       and my yet amazing gifts;
and so to commit back to you
   all of who I am,
     and all of who I'm not,
       then all the rest I'll never know,
        to find my rest in you.

Abide with me,
O God.

EL BEANS GRECO

There was a fury in her climbing, the edge of screech in her breathless muttering. "Sane? . . . Jezzus H . . . gimme a break! . . . What the . . . crap is sane? . . . Who in God's . . . half-acre . . . knows? . . . That zipper-assed . . . button-brain? . . . Gotta be . . . kidding . . . Scorches my buns . . . I ever gave . . . a fart's worth . . . of energy . . . trying to be . . . something . . . who the hell even . . . knows . . . for sure . . . what it . . . is! . . . Unfor . . . damn . . . giveable . . . waste!" She slipped, caught herself, and kept climbing. The rocks bruised her feet. The scrubby bushes scratched her. She stopped and yelled at them. At the rocks: "SPOILED IDIOTS! I'VE HAD ENOUGH OF YOUR DAMN TANTRUMS. KNOCK IT OFF!" At the bushes: "WHO DO YOU THINK YOU ARE, THE CRÈME DE LA CRÈME? YOU'RE JUST OVERGROWN WEEDS, SO GET YOUR ACT TOGETHER OR I'LL TURN YOU INTO SO MUCH . . . MULCH."

Completely winded by her outburst, she plopped down on a large rock. When she'd finally caught her breath, she resumed her conversation with the landscape: "Sorry if I disturb you, but God knows you have time enough to do nothing. Besides, I just have to . . . to . . ." She didn't know how to say it.

Suddenly she stood, turned toward the mountain top and exposed a long, red, still fresh scar where her left breast had been. She screamed, "FIRST YOU ALLOWED THIS, AND THEN I ALLOWED IT TO INTIMIDATE ME. I TOOK IT AS PUNISHMENT, AND I WAS TOO DAMNED GRATEFUL JUST TO HAVE SURVIVED IT. THAT WAS WRONG." Tears flooded down her face. "Wrong, wrong, wrong." Her voice choked into squeals and snorts of rage, grief, shame. Shortly words began to come in short bursts: "TAKE . . . TH'OTHERONE . . . TOO . . . IFTHAT'S . . . TH'WAY . . . ITHAST'BE . . . BU'THATISN'T . . . GONNASTOPME . . . ANYMORE . . . I'MCOMIN' . . . AFTERYOU . . . LIKEBEFORE."

The gravel shifted under her foot, and she fell awkwardly to her knees. She felt a quick rush of embarrassment, as she had when Sam Pratt had lectured her in front of the children. She tossed her head defiantly, sat heavily and, ignoring her skinned knees, growled, "Hell with retirement. Shove it, Pratt."

She picked up a stone, began rubbing it, giving it orders. "Listen up! You just tell your friends not to get in my way from here on. It's hard enough to be climbing way up here where it's so damn steep and cold without them making it harder for me." She spit on the stone and rubbed harder to bring out its hidden colors. "Besides, I've got to keep going and my feet hurt like hell already. So you tell 'em, hear?" She tossed the stone over her shoulder as far as she could. "By the way, tell 'em I love 'em, too."

She chuckled, got to her feet, rebuttoned her sweater, blew her nose as she'd learned to as a kid from the men building the street in front of her house: leaning over, finger against one nostril, exhaling mightily through the other nostril, letting the stuff fly to the ground; repeating on the other nostril, ending with a wipe on the sleeve. Bowing with a flourish to her surroundings, she said, "Thank you very much. Glad you liked it."

If anyone had seen or overheard her, they would have unquestionably doubted her sanity. Their doubt would not have surprised her. Intuitively, she knew that it was as a test of their doubt — and of her own — that she was climbing Mt. Adams in mid-afternoon so early in the spring. She was after the One people gave the name God to, or whatever other name struck them for the insistent mystery of things. It was time for a showdown. Was she insane? Was the world? Was God? She hitched up her bra strap and grunted more or less toward the mountain top, "Okay, here I come! Get ready!" And with a lurch she started to climb again.

* * * * *

They'd been looking for her for a half hour or more. A teacher who disappears on a school outing is quickly missed, especially if she's the oldest teacher in the school, just had an altercation with the principal, and stalked off in tears. At first the teachers assumed she'd gone to be alone in one of the little stone restrooms of the state park where they'd brought the youngsters for a scientific field trip and first-of-the- season picnic. When that proved wrong, they assumed she'd gone for a walk nearby. While they waited for her return, they gathered in little groups to gossip about what had happened, careful to not let the students overhear, their attempted protection only intensifying the young peoples' nibbling anxiety.

Miss Marshall, fifth grade Basic Science teacher, seemed to be the most vocal, if not the best informed, of one circle. "Everyone knows she's . . . well, eccentric is putting it mildly. Crazy is more like it. Like from another planet. My God, we've had to deal with it for years."

"That's a little harsh," observed Lisa Springer, who taught Social Studies. "Kirby's got spirit. Good for morale. Except she's seemed pretty down since her mastectomy. I worry about her."

"All the more reason for her to put it to rest," insisted Leah Marshall. "Feeling sorry for her doesn't change anything, really. How many times have we tried to tell her, as gently as we could, that it was time to give it up, retire, rock the grandchildren? But, no, not her. And now this. It's too much. Something just has to be done."

Some of the other teachers nodded, less in agreement than in encouragement, wanting diversion, curious about which tidbits of information floating about were most enticing. Leah Marshall indulged them. "Can you imagine, just when we're starting serious, scientific sex education, she has the gall to tell the children that ants mate inside daffodils at night, that she actually has observed the phenomena many times."

"Observed the phenomena? Get real! Whatever she said, I'm sure she didn't put it that way." It was Joe Straus, who taught computers and delighted in needling Leah Marshall.

Leah Marshall's tone became combative. "Well, *I* put that way! For God's sake, think of the damage it could do to the school if it got out that one of our teachers was spreading that kind of garbage around."

"Oh, I don't know. I bet X-rated biology would be a big hit." Other teachers laughed at Joe Straus' humor.

Leah Marshall didn't join the laughter. "Oh great, make a joke of it. That's really professional. But if you give a damn about education, as I perhaps have wrongly assumed we all do, then you can't ignore that kind of thing. And before you blow it off so lightly, just remember that Sam Pratt thought he had to check it out when he heard the kids talking about it. In fact, some of them wanted to stay here after dark so they could watch the ants, well, 'do it,' as they put it."

Joe Straus smiled and winked. "Maybe if we stayed after dark, they could watch more than the ants 'do it.' What do you say, Leah?" This time the rest of the group laughed even louder.

"Miss Marshall?" The laughter stopped abruptly. While they'd been talking, one of the children had approached unnoticed and was standing at the edge of their gathering. Joe Straus hunched his shoulders up to his ears and muttered, "Damn."

"Why, Thelma, what do you want?" Leah Marshall's smile was too bright, her voice too sweet.

"Nothing, really, Miss Marshall. I . . . I mean, we were just wondering. Ants could mate inside daffodils, couldn't they?"

In a voice icily indignant, Leah Marshall set about to nip this bud of ignorance. "No, they couldn't, Thelma," she instructed, matter-of-factly. "Ants are a highly organized species. Each member of the colony has very specialized functions. Some ants lay eggs, in pre-arranged places in the colony. Other ants fertilize the eggs, and the eggs turn into larvae which . . ."

"Miss Kirby told us all that," Thelma interrupted, "but she said that sometimes some ants get tired of that and go off to start something different. She said they're the ones who 'do it' . . . I mean, mate, in daffodils. That could be true, couldn't it?"

"Maybe it could be, Thelma." It was Joe Straus, kneeling to put his arm around the girl whose lip had begun to tremble. "Maybe it could." Leah Marshall snorted and turned away.

* * * * *

In another small group Sam Pratt's explanations were trying to grind away the rough edges of what had happened. "You know I have tried to be patient. Helen Kirby should have retired three years ago, but I kept her on."

"Come on, Sam," the music teacher, Elaine Fisher, countered, "she *could* have retired, not *should* have. Our contract says Administration can't force teachers to retire early."

Sam bristled. "I don't happen to agree with everything in that contract."

"That's your prerogative," Elaine Fisher replied. "Hers was not to retire. So cut the condescending crap about being so patient."

"Whether you know it or not, I have been very patient, Elaine," Sam snarled through clenched teeth. "To say that Helen Kirby has been less than cooperative is an understatement. For at least the past two year she has challenged every procedural change, every decision I've made."

Elaine Fisher chuckled. "*Every* decision, Sam? Surely you decided how many pencils to buy, who the new secretary would be, when to go to the john without Kirby challenging it." The other teachers smiled.

Sam ignored the comment. "The fact is that I . . . well, I just made the best of things. In fact, I did keep her on, even though it cost me a lot of aggravation. In all fairness, surely you've noticed how strange she's been acting, more so all the time?" The teachers diverted their eyes, resigning themselves to Sam Pratt's need to talk because they were almost as afraid as he was.

Sam raced on, trying to stay in control. "In any case, today was just inexcusable. When I overheard Johnny Toffer telling his friends what she'd said about ants 'doing it' in daffodils, I thought I should ask him about it. Then I marched them off to confront Helen Kirby and believe it or not all she could say was, 'Sam, have you ever looked inside a daffodil in the middle of the night? How do you know what's going on in there?'

"That did it. Wouldn't even admit it was an ill-advised joke. Humiliated me in front of the children. It was absolutely unprofessional behavior for a teacher, and I considered it my duty to deal with it on the spot or the children would have lost all respect for authority. You can see that under the circumstances, I didn't have any choice."

Again, the teachers diverted their eyes. O.D. McKeel, director of physical education, said softly, "You do remember she's had major surgery not too long ago, don't you?"

"I'm her principal, not her chaplain," Sam answered before turning and walking away.

Elaine Fisher noticed a clump of daffodils by the pump house and wondered if they were a wild variety or if someone had planted them there. She also wondered where Helen Kirby was.

* * * * * *

Some of the sixth grade class were having their own conference. "Look, if you saw her go that way, you gotta tell 'em, dorkhead." Nick Alveres was turning his fear into aggressive insistence.

Betty Schuster was dubious. "But if I tell and she went some other way, or if she just comes back, I'll be totally embarrassed, grossed out."

"Tell 'em!" Nick was firm. No one disagreed.

So Betty went to Mr. Pratt. "Mr. Pratt, somebody said they saw Miss Kirby going up that trail marked 'Summit.' We went to find her, but we couldn't."

The knot in Sam Pratt's stomach twisted up to his face. Sweat beaded on his upper lip. "Damnit!" he gasped. "Come on," he shouted to the others, turning and running up the trail, calling, "Helen! Helen Kirby!" Joe Straus, Elaine Fisher, and O.D. McKeel followed.

Within fifteen minutes they came back. "We have to call the State Police," Joe Straus announced. "No sense kidding ourselves that it's just a school matter anymore." Sam Pratt looked as if he was in shock. Some of the smaller children began to cry. The wind seemed to stir in apprehension. Everyone looked through the trees toward the summit, bleached to a remove by the afternoon light, inscrutable to their inquiring eyes.

* * * * *

She leaned against the big rock, the sun in her eyes, and squinted. The wind sniffed and teased her hair, as a cat teases before pouncing. She faced the mountain top and yelled, between gasps, "OKAY, YOU . . . YOU MISCREATOR . . . HOW D'YA . . . LIKE THAT WORD? . . . MISCREATOR! . . . SO YOU MADE THE WHOLE . . . THING . . . HOORAY FOR YOU . . . BUT YOU . . . MESSED UP . . . I KNOW YOU'RE THERE . . . I CAN SEE YOU . . . COME DOWN . . . CLOSER WHERE . . . WE CAN . . . SETTLE A . . . FEW THINGS . . ."

She coughed, gasped, breathed deeply for a minute. Then, almost to herself, she added softly, "And don't tell me you can't come down here. I've seen you all my life, hide-and-seeking around every damn corner I ever got into, every damn body I ever ran into, the near dying ones same as the just born ones. Even in this bitching thing." Her fingers kneaded the still unfamiliar vacancy on her left chest as if trying to coax the remaining flap into rising again. "You're nervy, all right. Hide and seek until most people give up seeking, almost like that's what you had in mind all the time. Well, you're not getting away with it with me."

She wiped her hand across her mouth. Her throat was so dry. She scooted around to the shadow side of the rock, got a hand full of snow, and began munching on it. Slowly, she worked her way back to the sunny side, and bellowed again: "THIS IS BEANS . . . YOU HEAR? . . . BEANS KIRBY . . . YOU'RE THE . . . one's RESPONSIBLE for . . . me having . . . that NICKNAME . . . SO LISTEN up . . . I'm TIRED of . . . TRYing to . . . live between . . . the lines." Her already hoarse voice had sunk to almost a whisper. She began remembering. The shadows moved quietly, steadily up the mountain.

* * * * *

The state police and the park rangers responded professionally, dividing the area into sections, marking maps, passing out equipment, beginning the search. More wood was gathered and fires were started in the picnic area. Two officers with a radio kept track of the search parties as they reported in, marking red Xs on a map laid out on a picnic table.

Parents were notified, and many came to pick up their children, but most children insisted they wouldn't leave until Miss Kirby was found. So the parents joined the vigil along with most of the teachers. Only a few children and teachers went back in a school bus. Typically, the teachers organized the fire tending, coffee making, and distribution of the food that kept appearing.

Such is penance: vague guilt seeking relief in concrete sound and movement. People talked, small talk trying to fill the craters of uncertainty and stave off the silences in which fear often breeds. Birds twittered noisily in the woods. Sam Pratt wondered if there had been so many of them before

* * * * *

It seemed as if "Beans" had always been her name. When she was a child, people laughed when she reported that she'd seen something they hadn't. On one such occasion, in those days of milder language, someone had said, "Ah, you're full of beans." The name had stuck, provoking more laughter. At first, she'd cried and asked, "What are you laughing at?" When no acceptable answer had been forthcoming, that question had become the core of her argument with God. Was she so different? Was she crazy?

In fourth grade her teacher had said to her mother, "Mrs. Kline, I think Helen may have problems with, well, her . . . vision. We suggest you have her checked."

Dutifully, her mother had taken her to the doctor where she had read the whole chart down to the last line of tiny letters, at which point the doctor had reassured her mother, "Well, that's excellent. Helen's eyes seem to be fine, Mrs. Kline."

Helen had protested, "But, Dr. Parke, there are things on the chart you didn't point to."

The doctor had frowned. "There are?" he asked. "Tell me about them, Helen." His tone and her mother's worried look had made her hesitate. Even now, across all the years, she could still feel that moment, could still see every detail in that office and smell the ominous silence.

Finally, she'd gone on. "Well, down in the corner it says, 'American Optical Co.' And all around the edges are white birds, only they have butterfly wings and wrinkled faces like grandmother's, and on their backs are children except they have shiny blue skin and eyes all orangy like the sun going down and . . ."

"Helen, stop that!" Her mother was shaking her.

Helen had been stunned. She had thought maybe they'd like what she could see. Instead, her mother had begun to cry, and the doctor had made her follow a little light around with her eyes, and after while he had suggested that her mother take her to another doctor.

In a few days they had gone to another doctor, and he'd asked her all kinds of questions and made her put different shaped blocks in different shaped holes and draw pictures. Finally, the doctor had asked quietly, "Helen, do you ever think you see things other people don't see?"

Strangely, she'd wanted desperately to talk about that with someone she could trust, but there didn't seem to be anyone like that in her life. So now when the doctor had asked the question, she knew how she'd better answer it.

"No," she'd insisted, "I only really see what everyone else sees. Sometimes I . . . imagine things . . . for fun, is all."

Her mother had smiled, the doctor had nodded and said, "I thought so. But you're much too grown up for that now. It's time to stop it. I know you will, for everyone's sake." He had turned to her mother. "Helen's fine, Mrs. Kline. As an only child she just has an active imagination she'll soon outgrow. No need to worry." That settled it for everyone.

Everyone except her. What she'd learned was that there were lines — top, sides, bottom — and that was it. It was dangerous to see or talk of anything existing outside those lines. People laughed, frowned, threatened, shook you if you did. They accused you of being full of . . . beans.

She opened her eyes and blinked away the memory. Above her, the mountain seemed to have become a gigantic flame silently sucking into itself the violet sky in which soared a great bird whose wings were dazzlingly white.

"Oh, God," she whispered, "if you don't break our hearts one way, you break them another. It's just too beautiful." Hoarsely she shouted, "IT'S NOT FAIR, YOU NUDNICK. COME AND MEET ME NOW." The bird and the violet slowly circled down.

* * * * *

Juanita Gomez had named her first son, Greco, after the Spanish painter El Greco, whose paintings she'd so admired when she went with her high school class to the museum, gone with Hector afterward, and ended up pregnant. Now Greco was himself just fourteen, finishing eighth grade, the oldest of eight, forced to make his own way in school and on the streets as well as into the puzzlement of a deepening voice, darkening mustache, and hazards of manhood.

Without understanding why, or asking if he could, Greco had begun hanging around Beans. She, in turn, had become attached to him, encouraging his interest in drawing, for which he showed talent, "as you should with a name like Greco," she'd say. When he had visited Beans in the hospital after her surgery, he had sensed that it had to do with more than just the loss of a breast, which seemed quite frightening enough to his young, erotic fascination with female anatomy. What more it had to do with, he struggled unsuccessfully to piece together from Beans' moody silences and his own churning emotions.

He would sit by her hospital bed for long stretches, sketching the ward, the nurses, the other patients, but mostly Beans lying in various positions on the bed. Invariably the left side of his sketches of her body were tentative, vague, one or two charcoal strokes scarcely touching the section of grainy white that he left as its own indecipherable message. Beans would look at his sketches, smile softly, and say nothing. The ache and the longing in him to understand what was happening to her, and to him, grew sharper even after she'd been discharged and resumed teaching again.

When a search party of park rangers set off in what he was sure was the right direction, Greco followed them. He grew quickly impatient with their progress. After all, he'd heard someone say that time was critical, Miss Kirby's age being what it was. Finally, running toward the slowly advancing party, he yelled, "She isn't lost. She went straight to the top. She always told me the mountain top is where God . . ." He stopped. "Look, just get your asses to the top, and maybe you'll find her before . . ." He stopped again.

The rangers had turned so quickly when he yelled that they almost lost their footing. Irritated, one of them spoke brusquely, "Damnit, who are you and what are you doing here?"

"Doesn't matter. I'm just telling you, you gotta get to the top quick or it'll be too late. You don't, I swear I'll bring a load down on your asses. Sue your asses off. Go on! Hustle!" His voice cracked. "Please?"

They stared at him, disbelieving, hostile. Finally, the one who had spoken earlier said, "Jake, why don't you and Ed go on up? The rest of us will keep the search going here." He studied Greco for a moment and then spoke with disarming softness, "Now, you get back down to the park with the other kids, or I'll have to report you for impeding law officers in the line of duty." In answer, Greco turned and ran up the trail past Jake and Ed. Behind him he heard the ranger call out, "Okay, stay with him, you guys."

Quick tears blurred Greco's vision, and the antiseptic smell of the mountain giddied him. He stumbled, caught himself. "Please, God, help me. I've got to get to her." Squinting toward the sky, he glimpsed a white blur out of which seemed to come a long finger, beckoning him on. He tried to wipe the tears from his eyes. Was it a sign from God? Or was it only a bird, or the slant of light from the sinking sun?

* * * * *

The nip of cold and darkness herded people closer to the fire where they sipped their coffee, spoke to each other as if to themselves, plucked at the frayed ends of their anxiety, mentioned the need for prayers they seemed to hope others knew better than they how to make. The children's prayers were in the wideness of their eyes and silences. They loved Beans.

Now a few of the adults were realizing that they loved her, too. On the boundary of shadow and firelight, they felt, rather than thought, something about themselves that they otherwise denied, yet somehow needed to have affirmed. Beans had been that affirmation. In her they had seen, if only dimly and as provocation for guilty ridicule, a possibility for themselves of a passion, a mating of dream and daring, spirit and claw, battle cry and love song, that, without their having to risk their consent, might be magically unleashed to force them out of the choke of their rutted definitions into a kind of ecstasy.

But the gravity of pay checks and social convention had been too strong. They'd followed society's proper lectionaries and prayed religion's well-worn prayer books while Bean had at it with God, or whatever was the mystery or the glory that made some people go mad. Secretly, they'd loved her for that. Secretly, they'd vowed that someday they'd get around to having at it, too. Meanwhile, she kept the possibility alive for them. Now the looming danger of her situation had pushed them a stumble closer to getting around to it. That added to their discomfort, which they relieved with talk.

Bits of conversation floated upward with sparks from the fire:

"Did you know she'd been married once?"
"I guess I did. Her husband die?"
"No. It ended. She never said why. Only that it broke her heart."
"Thought she lived with a woman."
"Did for a long time. Artist friend. Had a studio together."
"Think she's a lesbian?"   "I don't know."
"She always said it was love that mattered, not a lot of stupid rules."
"Sounds too easy. Too self-serving."
"Not the way she went at it."

"Or the way she insisted God goes at it."

"The way she went at it didn't seem to get her much, did it?"

"Depends on what you mean by much, I guess."

"Anyway, who knows how God goes at anything?"

"Or if God goes at anything."

"I don't know."

"Maybe lovers know. A little."

"You mean safe-sex lovers, of course."

"Come on. I mean . . . oh, you know what I mean, for Christ's sake."

"I do?"   *"Yes, you do!"*

*"Beans was always saying that love is all of a piece.
Said teaching can be making love."*

"You think her mastectomy changed her?"

"Made her a little quieter is all."   *"I mean about love."*   *"No."*

"You should have heard her teach the kids about wild flowers today."

"Yeah?"

*"Made a game of it. She'd give the Latin name for a
flower and have them guess what color marker to draw it
with on their pads."*

"Really?"

*"Yeah! She'd say, 'Ranunculus.' Kids had to figure out yellow, for
buttercup. 'Lobelia cardinalis.' Red, for cardinal flower. Then she
said, 'Podophyllum. Most mysterious color of all.' Kids were stumped
for a minute. Beans started laughing and said, 'Come on, you
know. White, for May apple.' Kids howled, 'No fair. That's no color,
Miss Kirby.' Beans howled back, 'It's every color. That's why it's so
mysterious, dummies.' Kids laughed. One of 'em started chanting,
'Po-do-phyl-lum, po-do-phyl-lum.' The others joined right in; 'po-do-
phyl-lum, po-do-phyl-lum.' It was great."*

"Probably be something they'll never forget, all right."

"Do you think she's right about love?"   *"Guess she might be close."*

"I know Beans touched something in me all my years of therapy didn't."

"You think she's all right? I mean, she's not off the deep end or anything?"

No one answered. They sat quietly and watched the sparks from the fire ascend to become the evening star.

* * * * *

Beans Kirby leaned one hand against a rock, head cocked, and studied the mountain, tinted shades of violet against the deepening purple of the sky. She shifted her gaze to where, 1500 light years away, a faint Orion bestrided the heavens. Orion was there, in space, yet it swirled inside her brain; there, fifteen hundred light years away, but here, where she stood looking; here, in her, even when she closed her eyes; then, yet now. How could time be visible, sensual? But it was. It was real as a lover, in her eyes, on her skin, in her body.

Her sight felt, listened, touched. In the scarlet edges of the setting sun, she could see the green ray throb from it for a second or two. She could see the wind, vibrations of particles in the air even when no leaf betrayed its presence. She could see the longings of people though they did not speak of them even to themselves. Was the gift her eyes, or what they saw? What was real? Who was sane? What were human beings anyway?

She turned and lay back against the rock, hard as a pew. She smiled and recalled when she was young, going to church, where she'd heard the wonderful stories of those six-winged, flaming-faced seraphim who screamed terrible, holy, wild things. But no one ever screamed terrible or wild things of agony or ecstasy in church except the evangelists who came through and seemed to do it on cue like the rock singers the kids liked so much these days. And church had never let silence get heavy enough to stagger anyone into anything very deep, or awesome, or joyful either. Church was all lines, too: pews, candles, hymns, creeds, plastic cups of juice, even the Bible readings. It was a bore.

She laughed and shouted, "HEY, I KNOW YOU'RE THERE. YOU CAN'T HIDE IN THE DARK OR THE SILENCE. YOU DON'T LEAVE ME ALONE SO I . . ." her voice cracked, ". . . won't . . . let you . . . alone." She sucked in air, went on. "I'M not . . . AFRAID . . . I DON'T . . . believe . . . death . . . is the . . . bottom . . . LINE . . . I SPit . . . at it." She hawked, spit, began to cough, and dropped on her side. When the coughing eased, she whispered, "Go ahead, fight dirty, but I warn you I'm one of those meshuggenehs who won't let go 'til you give me a blessing."

She rolled over on her back and looked into the deepening darkness. Around the lower edge of the sky was a much lighter rim of purple, and at the very center of the overhead dome was an eerie light, as though someone had poked a hole to let in the radiance of some far off sun.

"All right," she whispered, "I know how to be quiet about terrible, wondrous things. But before it's too late, I DEMAND YOU . . . or ONE OF YOUR BUMbling assistants," she started coughing again, ". . . tell . . . me . . . whose lines . . . who drew . . . them . . . in the first place?"

Paroxysms of coughing ripped through her, echoing in a hundred hidden caverns, clefts, and fissures of the mountain, which seemed to transpose it into laughter.

The stars watched silently, but a thousand feet further up the mountain, a white-winged bird raised its head from a bit of carrion and lifted majestically into the descending night. Below, a field mouse dove for its hole.

* * * * *

"Tell me why the stars do shine . . ." One of the parents was leading the children in camp songs. Some of the search parties had straggled back into the picnic grounds. Earlier optimism became only half-believed, and assurances were frequently repeated: "Someone will find her . . . Don't worry." Then the silence was filled with even more silent prayers, and the sound of little creatures scampering in the woods, and whatever causes dry branches to break, and the indecipherable messages of the wind.

* * * * *

"Damnit, get a move on. Hustle!" Greco was driven by a terrible urgency. He would have left the rangers behind except they had the essential flashlights

"How do you know we didn't go right past her in the dark?," Ed panted.

"I just know," Greco yelled. "Come on. Enough of your damn resting every two minutes." He turned and started toward the top.

Jake groaned. "Tough keeping up with this kid. Gotta remember to thank Scotty for this assignment." He and Ed got to their feet and went after Greco.

Greco looked back to see if they were coming, then glanced up. Something was moving in the dark sky. It was the white blur again. Was it an angel? If so, was it of life or of death? The blur soared off like a glider. Do birds fly at night? Greco wondered. Was it a bat of some kind? Had the others seen it? "Come on, hurry," he called over his shoulder.

Suddenly from the distance came the sound of something like laughter. The three men froze. "What the hell was that?" Jake shouted.

* * * * *

Her coughing had stopped. She shuddered, gasped. A searing pain ripped through her chest, the weight of it surprising her, pinning her to the ground for what seemed an eternity. Finally, she managed to rasp through clenched teeth, "So this . . . is how you . . . honor . . . my promise . . . to be quiet? . . . Take away . . . the cough . . . give pain." It took enormous effort to roll on her side, pull her knees into a fetal position. The pain eased.

Slowly, she uncurled. "This is . . . how . . . you come?" she panted. "Well, it's not . . . so bad . . . the pain." Carefully, she rolled onto her back and tried to use her sleeve to wipe the sweat from her face. The pain flared, subsided again when she lowered her arm. "Neither is . . . the quiet . . . ness," she said after a moment.

Overhead the stars began to spin. She felt herself spinning with them. It was a pleasant, floating, peaceful feeling. She closed her eyes, smiling, panting. Her lips began to move, the sound they shaped was almost too soft to hear. "Ah . . . the lines . . . aren't . . . what we think . . . are they?" Quietness cradled her. As in a dream, she began to hum fragments of a tune, a hymn, bits of words out of distant memory, "mmmm . . . 'more light' mmm . . . 'and' mm . . . 'truth' . . . mmm 'to break' . . . mmm 'forth' . . . mm 'from' mmmm . . . "The humming ceased for a long moment. Again her lips barely moved. "Always . . . more." Gradually her breathing slowed and she seemed to sleep.

Suddenly her eyes opened as if someone had startled her awake. Somehow she managed to push herself to her knees where she began to hum and sway, extending her hands as if holding out the corners of a gown, an apron, her eyes staring off to a distant time, another place. She spoke surprisingly loudly, clearly, as if to someone at whom she smiled, "Yes, I . . . always dared . . . to see . . . far as . . . I . . . you . . . able . . . me . . . to . . ."

She swayed now, on the mountain, in her kitchen, on her lover's bed, on her knees with children, with a partner at a dance, catching in her outstretched filmy garment shards of starlight, galaxies of time, scents of creation itself — mud, stone, silence, sea, word and relationship, love and pain, choice and failure, joy and . . . beyond. Then the wonder of it burst inside, gently drifting through her like an afterglow.

"Well . . . hello . . . again," she whispered into the translucent darkness. "I . . . been . . . expectuugh . . ." A bubble in her throat turned her words to a gurgle, " . . . 'ove 'ou." She pitched forward and turned slowly face up. A flake of snow crystallized on her forehead, first of thousands that began to fall — white, trembling, peaceful.

* * * * *

Greco willed himself to find her before the snow forced the rangers to call off the search, as they were already threatening to do. Just as Jake yelled to him, "Hey kid, it's hopeless; we gotta go back," he spotted her, ran, gathered her in his arms, brushed the snow from her face.

"Beans," he implored, "Beans." He'd never called her that.

She opened her eyes for a flicker, smiled, whispered, "Pretty . . . fresh . . . Greco." Her chuckle came out a weak cough. Her breathing was labored.

"Come on, Beans, you're gonna make it," Greco almost shouted at her.

As if fighting sleep, she tried to open her eyes but they refused to stay open. Greco pressed his cheek against hers. She whispered, "You . . . painter . . . El . . . Greco's . . . right . . . Proportions . . . are . . . different . . . n' . . . we . . . think . . . Don't . . . forget . . . okay?"

Greco's tears were warm between their cheeks. "Won't ever forget, Beans. Promise." He rocked her gently. "O God," he whispered, "O God, God, God!" When at last he loosened his embrace to look at her, the flashlights of the rangers who stood quietly behind him turned her snow-laced hair into a glowing corona. This time it was Greco's lips moved almost silently, "Podophyllum."

* * * * *

They took her down in a canvas body bag as off a battlefield: down past the wild daffodils; down past the watchful, tearful eyes in the picnic area; down past the children who, one after another, reached out to touch her still form. Past blind guilt or bitterness or sorrow, they saw with primitive intuition the terrible, wonderful way things do mate, come together, create life in staggering, awesome dimensions, unnoticed and uncelebrated except by the mad, the imaginative, the faithful.

Down she came from the mountain heights from which covenants, visions, mysterious powers had come through the ages, streaming life and renewed struggle in their wake. Down she came, feet first, the head of her shroud carried by Greco who, oblivious to whoever might overhear, kept up his dialogue with her: "I never understood what it was before, but you never really lost it after all, did you? All you lost was your, you know, . . . breast. Okay, bad enough, but not as bad as if you actually lost what mattered. That, you just misplaced for a while, right? I can dig that. Actually, if you hadn't, maybe I wouldn't have, you know, come to see it a little for myself. Like one artist to another, you might say. El Beans Greco, like you said. I suppose it'll drive some people crazy, huh? Including me, right? Yeah, right."

He started to laugh, but it turned to a lump in his throat. His eyes teared up. There was a jolt on the bag that almost caused one of his hands to lose its grip. Clearing his throat, he said with a kind of fierce tenderness, "Hey, watch it. Watch it down there."

Rehearsals for the eternal

O Lord,
    your word creates;
    my words stumble after,
        resonant, echoing, reflecting,
            sharing small bits of power;
    but finally they're too frail
        to climb the sunlit heights
            of my own resplendent life,
        or walk its more barren plateaus,
            or plumb its ugly, shadowed depths,
                or even accurately form your name,
    though I must use them, just the same,
        to try,
            as you have created me to do.

So hear me, "I will be what I will be,"
    Lord, Jehovah, Yahweh, Elohim,
        Christ, Father, Mother, Holy Spirit,
            Alpha, Omega, One, God beyond God,
    hear these words that stumble after
    and would help me be with you.

This life your word has given me
    is such a strange, yet common gift,
        so fraught with twists and storms,
            betrayals, mercies, inspirations,
                revelations, hidden leaven
                    raising the daily to given bread.
    There is pain in it, sometimes,
        oft loneliness, riddles and enigmas,
            wounds endured, inflicted
                beyond the screaming of them,
                    and terrors I can't name,
    yes, and glories, too,
        seen, heard, felt,
            borne, beyond all telling —
    save by praise
        my frail words cannot raise to heaven,
            but fills a corner
                of my heart.

O God,
　　by your word you take away,
　　　　as if you're creating by corrosion,
　　　　　　by the astringent acid of grace,
　　shrinking slowly, sometimes, always painfully,
　　　　those too believable illusions,
　　　　　　which are temptations in disguise,
　　　　　　　　that I could be more than I am —
　　　　　　　　　　mortal being not enough —
　　　　　　by virtue of hard work,
　　　　　　　　that ultimate of ethics
　　　　　　　　　　by which even you are measured,
　　　　　　　　　　　　and usually found wanting,
　　　　　　　　　　　　　　by the way,
　　　　　　　　since I, among the we,
　　　　　　　　　　want more mountains moved
　　　　　　　　　　　　and mysteries solved.
　　Surely power for such marvels must be gained religiously
　　　　by the exercise of discipline,
　　　　　　the zeal of right believing,
　　　　　　poetic prayer,
　　　　　　arguing like a prophet,
　　　　　　a hunter's love, a schemer's hope,
　　　　　　the faith of sound investors,
　　　　　　the thousand ways to work at immortality
　　　　except . . .
　　　　　　slowly, in time, with age,
　　　　　　illusions atrophy, dissolve,
　　　　　　and the hard lesson is learned:
　　　　　　　　mortal limits are not breached
　　　　　　　　by mortal assaults, ethical or not.
My words are not all that's too frail,
　　O Thou beyond my names,
　　　　yet I'm more resonant for all of that,
　　　　　　and old enough to pray for grace,
　　　　　　　　and aching now to praise,
　　　　trusting that you'll hear my words,
　　　　　　having stripped my illusions away.

O God,
 I think of Christ
  and am made glad
   for this strange gift of life
    so strangely shared;
  glad for what can be broken,
   unbreakable would be less,
    broken but not destroyed —
     Jesus' life stories are
     the stories of my life;
  glad for your demonstrated promise
   of a love that follows after
    no matter where I run,
     finally to death itself;
  glad for your summons to do justly,
   to love mercy — seeing how I need it —
    to walk humbly with you
     and with this motley crew of brother, sister marvels,
      and to find joy in the walking, however far it goes;
  glad that what gets broken can be put together again,
   made new, some way,
    by sharp eyes, and brave, daring hands.
Help me, now and then, to measure myself
 not by my fears or failures,
  however large,
 but by my faith and hope and love,
  however small,
 that I may truly live this mortal gift
  and be a source of life
   for those I carry in my heart,
 and, by your grace,
  and naked to your presence,
 all my struggles, all my joys,
  will be daily rehearsals for the eternal,
   lessons in what it means
    to be human,
     finite,
      and yours.

RESURRECTION
MOMENTS

Solitary unconfinement

O God,
    in the darkness of night,
        grievance,
        worry,
        and regret,
    as I lay wrinkled with the sheets,
        alternating sweat and shiver,
        sighing my life away, again,
        despairing of even your existence,
        despondent over death's foul drool,
        sensing its snuffle in my every breath,
    an alert sounded in the closing vault of me,
        signal that the darkness was incomplete,
            strewn, as usual, with the lint of light
                caught here and there
                    on ceiling, wall, corner of bed,
            flicked away by unseen hand of wind,
                or brush of cloud, or whirl of earth,
                    but insistently strewn back again,
        widening the pupils of my eyes,
            unbidden by me,
                yet preparing them to learn,
                to watchful welcome.
Strange revelation,
    oft repeated, too often missed,
        spill of even more mysterious ones,
            but a kind of resurrection just the same,
                if taken as such,
                which I am.
My spirit opened, opens even now,
    the shreds of light the keys,
        and memory stirs from its vast store
            occasions, encounters, gifts
                which give life, bless it, keep it;
    and from my solitary unconfinement of prayer,
        gratitude emerges to return to you
            by sieve of words, the quickening of my spirit.

O God,
    I would remember on ahead
        the splendors lacing my daily round,
        parables at every common hand,
        essential things:
            the green-gold-stark turning of the seasons;
            parents who, as best they can, give life;
            children who, trusting it, enlarge it;
            mocking birds (I know of one) somehow taught to sing
                the first four resounding notes of Beethoven's Fifth;
            the smell of rain, the sensuous wetness of the trees;
            fierce-tender fathers, nursing mothers, Mother earth;
            poets, like prophets, bringing truth to bloody birth;
            friends who press past the confusing swing of my moods
                to confront and bless the struggles of my self;
            this lover here beside me linking fidelity to grace;
            that large otherness of things and life and you
                that keeps me, somehow, sometimes painfully,
                from being devoured in a frenzy of fancied virtues
                or proudly drowned in an intellectual tidal pool;
            moments of surprise, more than meager memory serves,
                when the cadences of my life
                    catch your rhythms
                and the spilt radiances of grace
                    license a curious seeing in the dark
    and turn my time to the slow, eternal setting
            of terror to peace,
                truth to music,
                    mercy to laughter,
                      hope to feast,
                        love to recreation,
                          me to resurrection.

Whetting of attention

O God,
	creator of life and death,
		there is something terrible,
			inviolable, holy
	not about death so much
		as the limits it sets,
			confronts us with,
				insists upon us
		so we cannot miss them
			because they do not miss us,
		and you who sets them
			like cherubim
				with flaming swords
					at the gates of Eden.

You are the Limiter,
	the over against,
		more than,
			not me,
	You —
		never owing anything,
			always giving something,
				forever promising everything,
					delivering resurrection,
						which is the miracle
							of every life, of mine.

So death comes,
	one way or another,
		and we gather around
			the mystery
				which is life.

O Limit Setter,
    that's death's gift, isn't it? —
        to gather us,
           to gather me
               with a kind of whetting of attention,
                    awareness honed on fear and praise.

Death comes,
    limits press,
        horizons compress
           to gather us,
           to gather me
               now, in the now, for the now,
           focusing,
           summoning me
               to end the compromising of my compromises,
               to take time before time takes me,
               to realize what matters,
               to grasp what I might be gathered for,
                   to look into an other's eyes,
                   to hold something close, put nothing off,
                   to make the choice, make it again,
                      to be a truth,
                      to be a mere marvel of a human being,
                      to dance a yes,
                      to slow the rush;
               to be gathered up in strength,
               to press on to that awesome passing on,
                   that "whatever" this mere marvel human being
                   must pass in and out and through
                      on the way from this limit of me
                      to that larger one of there and wherever
                      but never further, save by you;

by those rites of passage,
  passing rights,
    births, baptisms, graduations,
      weddings, funerals, worship —
       yes, worship most of all,
  to the life that I would get to,
   am called to but . . .
     must somehow die to reach.

Dying to something is the only way
  to get to anything that matters a lily's worth —
   dying to fear, guilt, pride, ambition,
    to pride of place which is no place,
     to a thousand vanities and martyrdom —
 and that's the unanxious love of it,
   isn't it, you setter of the limits
    we gather around to be raised beyond,
     raised out of that pursuit of Eden,
      that garden I am limited out of,
    to pass on toward a promised land,
     a garden east of Eden, a new Jerusalem.

So gather me now, O God,
  from the hundred hiding places
   my fear has spooked me into,
    that I might be free to live
     as one possessed
      by something larger than myself,
       by you, not limited by my limits,
   to live as one aware that the grace I seek
    is always seeking me,
     and all, including death itself,
      is grace gathering us to your self.

Only the light of you

O Christ,
    my friend is dying
        of something there's no cure for —
           mortality, of course —
    except his has more immediately
        terminal complications
           than mine . . . as far as I know.
    My friend's death is untimely
        which, I suppose, is really
           death's only way to be.
So it came to you,
    so it will come to me.
I'm sad, afraid, feeling helpless.

O Christ,
    how many more times
        must I stand by beds, graves,
           in rooms of grief,
               loneliness,
               outraged defeat,
               shriveling fear,
               anquished guilt
                   for not having loved well?
What can I do?
    I have loved no better,
        am no better lover,
           surely know no more,
               than those I stand with,
                   or would stand for.
    Good Lord, you know mortality,
        this dusty way I am,
           has its complications.
What is there to do?
    I'm no doctor,
        no genius of research,
           no skilled technician,
    just a friend,
        a mortal friend.

All I can do is pray —
    all there is to do, at last,
        probably at first as well,
            if any of us really knew.

O Christ,
    I'm ashamed at my relief
        that I'll survive my friend;
            I have no "greater love than this,"
                none close to half as great as yours,
and that's my confession, to begin with.

But then . . .
    there might be those for whom I'd die
        because I love,
            if dying would give them life,
so that's my hope and second confession.

Mortality is a heavy load, O Lord.
All I can do is pray out my tears, my faith.

O Christ,
    I pray for my friend;
        for healing, yes,
            but is that the miracle?
After all, how long would that be for?
I ask a deeper healing for him (and me),
    which is for you to be with him
        in some clear way he'll know
            (even though I'll know less clearly),
and so for peace,
    a readiness, an easy death,
        the fulfillment of your promise
            of no more pain nor tears nor night
                but only the light of you.
The strange thing is, O Lord,
    my friend has grown brave, these days,
        and free, and more alive, somehow;

every time I leave,
    he says, with a wan smile,
        "If I don't see you here,
            I'll see you there."

I pray this not so you will know,
    but so I might.
It is a kind of dimmer view,
    a curious intimation,
        an even stranger complication
        of this mortality.
Gratitude seems a poor mix with grief
    but there it is.

O Christ,
    I pray for me,
        and in the praying ask
            for courage, and for grace,
to wait no longer but to seize
        what always waits for me —
            life not death,
            this friend, and the others,
            a hand to clasp, a need to meet, and to have met,
            a word to speak, to hear, a tear to shed,
            a stand to take here and now, and for a then,
            bread to eat, wine to share, a mortal fool to be,
            and this decision to make,
                as now I do, and will again,
to give you what you want,
    which is accepting you
        in being who I am,
    and trusting you will raise in me
        what you will, at last,
            and will so in my friend.

O Christ,
    I entrust us to you.
        Please, let me die of nothing less
            than love, and giddy liveliness.

No verifiable fingerprints

O God,
    you touch everything, but lightly,
        leaving no verifiable fingerprints.
  In how many thousand quite unlikely, routine times,
      like a lucky changing of my mind
          and familiar, curious spaces,
      like the sacred meeting place of eyes,
          and ways of usual, odd coincidence,
      like the crucial key of shared insight
          (at once preserving my freedom and your lavish mystery),
  do you bear me as a father,
  guide me as a mother,
  captivate me as a child,
  challenge me as a friend,
  confront me as an enemy,
  ignore me as holiness having its own terms,
      which are not mine until this mortal's fears turn wiser . . .
        as now they slowly do?

O Elusive, Ingenious One,
    my dullness, doubt, even my death
      does not prevent you from being God,
        from touching everything lightly, even me,
        from ruffling my spirit like a quick breeze ruffles water,
    leaving me aroused and watchful now,
        waiting at the edge of love,
        praying hard for your return.

Come, Lord,
    for the easy sonnets of the day,
      the well-honed phrase, the well-learned prayer
        rattle empty as night falls
          and turn to mock my earlier charade.
  Your touch, and time, has shivered me to readiness,
      a mortal's quiet willingness,
        a listening, a gratitude,
          a quaking reliance on your promise of life
            in the haunting, risen Christ.

And yet, O God,
    this weight upon my heart, this stone,
        is too great for me to move alone.
    Come, roll it away:
        this crush of fear,
        this smother of self-preoccupation,
        this ponderous ego,
        this bloated arbiter of right,
        this bejeweled scepter of doubt;
   and raise me up in mercy,
        raise me up
            higher than the drag of past,
                higher than all present feeling,
   to trust that you
        will never give me up
            because of what my death
                would mean, not just to me,
                    but even more to you—
                    a child's death
                        to a Mother,
                        to a Father.

O trustworthy Friend,
   raise me up to trust like that,
      to love like that;
         and, perhaps a little past
            this dark glass of mortality
                in which I but dimly see,
      to glimpse, by bold imagination,
         a hallowed face, or fiery back,
            the making new a thing or two,
            a possible new me;
  and so, by grace, to come to life,
        and come to dare,
          and come to hope
            your future in.

O God, for Christ's sake,
        touch me, even lightly,
           once again and . . .
               it will be enough.

Caught up and crazed

Awesome God,
    be with me in this now that slips away,
       yet stretches toward forever,
    as you promised to be when you began
       the tolling out of time,
    for I can scarcely bear, and not alone,
       the mystery of my being.

I raised again from sleep this morn,
    or better, I was raised
       by some swish of light,
          some stir of who knows what,
    returned from that eerie float,
       half-remembering that no place.

I'm raised besotted with fragments,
    hauntings, strange hints, longings,
       buds of blessings, curious pieces —
          this unfinished puzzle that I am,
             undone work of you, cosmic puzzle maker;
    raised as out of that chaos I was made from
       on that first of your mornings,
          that beginning-out-of-nothing
             when the stars started their hum
                and there were shouts of joy,
    which I, yes, fearfully half-remember.

So raise me, again,
    with the quake of your passing train, and time's,
       from the stupor of inattention,
          dull repetition,
             my bleating as a victim,
                my quick, cowardly capitulation
                   to the bluffing of supposed fate;

and hold me for a timeless time
    in such deep holiness and peace
        that I may know that you are God,
    and find trust within my soul —
        trust being the only thing
            it truly knows, or needs to,
                to make the dare of life and prayer;
            love and hope,
                mercy and praise,
                    a dazzle of alertness
                        all come after.

Fill me with your spirit, O wondrous God,
    until I am unburdened, unhinged, undamned,
        caught up and crazed by something
            like glory, power, a tumult of marvels,
    and I will never be the same
        for being now with you.
Raise me to string this day
    on the thread of grace and courage,
to write it with such bloody truth
    as will withstand the lies;
to live it boldly, hold it precious,
    do it justice, love it gently;
and then to let it gladly go,
    to be carried somewhere to forever
        o'er the horizon into the night,
            onto storms and stars and sun,
                returning thus to you who gave it;
and in it learn —
    oh courage, God, to learn —
        this way of life fulfilled,
            this release of awe and peace,
                this trace of the unutterable,
                this resurrection rouse,
                    this risk of ecstasy.

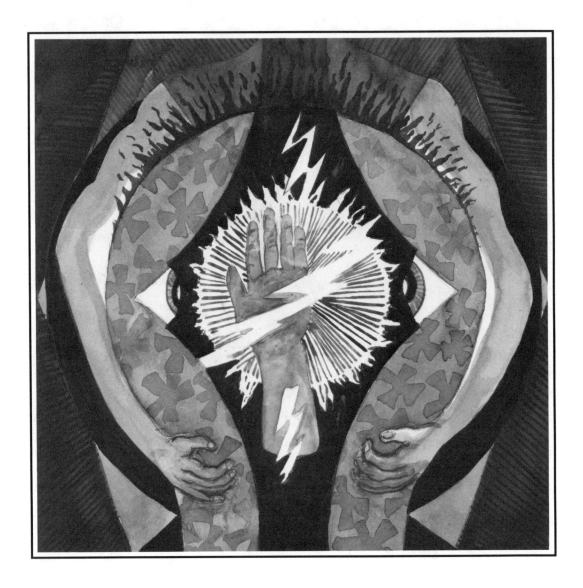

A GARDEN
THE OTHER SIDE OF EDEN

First was the sound of out-of-breath gasping as of someone running for his life. Then the gasping sucked into a grunt of great effort, exploded into a anguished scream, and deepened into a roar of outrage as the head of the old man's cane crashed into the crucifix on the wall and sent it spinning down the late-morning-nearly-empty hospital corridor. The old man, momentarily startled at what he'd done, watched the crucifix' flight in amazement, then felt a degree of relief that was close to vindication — and so to trust, strangely even to joy.

In that split second the crucifix blurred, became a trowel spinning into the box on his porch where he'd gotten good at tossing it on his way to washing his hands after gardening. That buzz of memory flickered into a smile on his lips as he lurched on down the corridor toward the startled people appearing in the doorways, summoned from their quiet duties by his frenzied one.

* * * * *

His heart had been in it at first. Not because he was particularly good at it, but because of the pleasure of it. He liked gardening. He thought of flowers as female, their color, scent, shape stirring him as beautiful women had stirred him when he had been a younger man — and stirred him still, though less urgently. He liked the pace of gardening. He liked his hands in the dirt, the feel of the sun, the breeze in his hair, the reassuring, slightly provocative smell of the earth. He liked the remembering, and forgetting, he was able to do as he planted, watered, weeded. He liked the pride he felt in turning the nondescript little plot in front of his small row house into a garden that, in his view, noticeably improved the neighborhood.

It had been early March when they'd moved in. Within a week, the impulse stirred in him. The second week it nudged him out into the front yard to dig up the small area between the sidewalk and the house. The third week he bought and mixed in mulch and fertilizer. Then he began planting things with no detailed plan but with much tenderness and hope.

When the various seeds and bulbs began to grow, he could hardly wait to get out in the garden each morning with his battered water bucket and the coffee can he used to dip out what he called "a little shot" for each plant. Frequently, he spoke to them as he moved from one to another. With a kind of shy longing, he sometimes even found himself talking to God as if God were another gardener. His heart was in it, at first.

* * * * *

Now, seven months later, he was rampaging down the third floor corridor of the east wing of St. Monica's hospital, swinging his cane at the crucifixes on the walls. The nurses and doctors scattered before him as if he were the carrier of a deadly, untreatable plague. A nurse crouched behind the nurses' station, one arm shielding her head as she yelled into the phone, "Hell, yes, it's a crisis. Tell security to get their asses up here before this frigging whacko kills someone. Damn sure, I mean it. This guy's . . ."

A crash interrupted her as a crucifix bounced off the counter into the computer screen behind the nurses' station. The the force of the old man's swing jerked his cane out of his hands, sending it ricocheting off the ceiling and into a stack of medical charts, bouncing them off the counter and onto the floor.

For the old man, the clatter coalesced into a single stab of pain. He felt as if his head was exploding and realized that his left arm and leg were uncontrollably jerking, his vision blurring. Yet, he heard and wanted desperately to protest the nurse's description of him but couldn't get the words from his brain to his lips. "Not a frigging whacko," was the slippery shred of consciousness he tried to hold on to as he stumbled toward the floor and darkness.

The "Code Blue" team and hospital security arrived on the scene at the same time. The man was diagnosed as having suffered a stroke and was hooked up to all the necessary life-support systems.

Security checked the identification in the man's wallet. His name was Ben Gregory, and there was an address. The head nurse on the floor called Admissions, which in turn called Social Services, to trace the man's family. There was no answer to repeated telephone calls.

Because Security couldn't explain how a crazy, unauthorized man had gotten onto a medical floor before visiting hours where he could endanger staff and patients, the circumstances were not only embarrassing to the hospital but also presented a potential liability. So a decision was made to send a case worker and a security guard to the man's address to talk to the family, if there was one, before bringing the police into the situation.

The security guard recognized the address as being in the neighborhood where he'd lived as a kid, near St. John's Church and its school, which he'd attended. He and the social worker found the house around the corner from the school.

As they waited for a response to their knock on the door, the social worker idly observed, "Great day, huh? Great month, October."

"Yeah," the security guard yawned.

"So you lived around here," the social worker went on, knocking on the door again. "Neighborhood's a little run down maybe, but nice enough. Wonder what happened to those flowers?" She pointed toward the garden in front of the house where chrysanthemums and marigolds lay trampled in the dirt.

"Kids, probably," the security guard shrugged.

The social worker thought of Ben Gregory's rampage through the hospital that morning and how he was lying unconscious now, hooked up to all those machines that were keeping him alive. In spite of the warm sun, she shivered and found herself hoping no one would answer the door. She stepped off the stoop and studied the garden. "Sort of like the world, in a way. Much as I work with people, I keep wondering what makes them do things like that — just destroy things."

"Come on, you know what goes down these days," the security guard replied. "Drugs 'n stuff. Dealers, pushers oughta be shot. Plus the damn kids, they think they c'n get away with anything. Oughta get their butts' kicked, most of 'em. Do time."

The social worker shook her head. "Yeah, drugs are a bitch, all right. Few jobs might help, though. But I wonder what made this Gregory guy break up the hospital like he did. What do you think set him off like that?"

The security guard was impatient. "Ask me, the guy's just psycho. Dangerous. Oughta be put away. Lucky nobody got hurt."

"No one but him, I guess," the social worker smiled sadly. She walked over to the trampled garden. Had something in Ben Gregory's brain begun to snap even before his stroke? Was that why he charged through the hospital knocking crucifixes off the wall? She smiled again in spite of herself. "I heard he knocked four crucifixes off the walls, smashed a statue of the Virgin, and ripped a painting of the Pope. Can you imagine that? It must have been quite a sight."

"Quite a sight? Crazy bastard might'a hurt somebody. He scared the hell outta people," the security guard retorted. "Oughta hav'ta pay damages to people, the hospital, for the whole damned mess."

"He probably did a better job scaring people than all the crucifixes," the social worker chuckled. When the security guard frowned, she quickly added, "Sorry, no offense meant. There's something funny about it, though. I know it'll take time for security to live it down, but I still can't help wishing I'd seen it when the orderly got so scared he tipped over the bedpans on the cart on the way to emptying them. It must have been a riot, right?"

"Guy should'a been put away a long time ago," the security guard answered without a smile.

The social worker gave up. "I guess no one's here. I suppose we should check with some of the neighbors."

"Yeah," the security guard agreed.

As she turned from the garden, the social worker sighed, "What a shame. I'll always wonder what makes people do things like that."

"I told ya," the security guard argued, "people got no sense of morals, no respect for law and order these days."

"Like you do?" the social worker asked.

"Yeah, as a matter of fact. Like me," the guard insisted. "Sure wasn't anybody like me messed up that garden."

The social worker shrugged. "No, I suppose not. Come on, let's go."

* * * * *

Ben and Nora had bought the house to be near her son, Mason, his wife, and small child. It had been a mistake. Since Ben and Nora were older, everyone assumed they were married, but they weren't. Both Nora, whose complete name was Nora Pettibone Cunningham, and Benjamin Alexander Gregory were retired on small pensions and social security. They liked each other, enjoyed being together, and decided it would be beneficial in many ways, including financially, if they lived together. The catch was they couldn't marry or Nora would lose her pension and other benefits. So they made their peace with their consciences and took the risk. But what seemed an acceptable arrangement for young people was much less so for older ones.

When they moved into the city, Nora's son wanted nothing to do with them, insisting that their arrangement was "filthy, rotten, immoral." Actually, for Mason Cunningham, their arrangement had less to do with their morality than with his fear of exposure. He was afraid his campaign for city alderman would be in serious trouble if his opponents discovered what his mother was doing and made it an issue.

"I'm running to make the city better," Mason argued in a voice loud enough to force his mother to hold the telephone away from her ear, thus enabling Ben to overhear. "And what kind of stupid trick does my own mother pull on me? Threat of scandal, that's what. Could ruin my career, everything I'm trying to do. It's outrageous what you and that . . . that pimp of yours are doing. Plus, he got you to put all your savings into that place, didn't he? For godsake, Mother, you must'a gone senile or something."

Ben lost it and screamed back, "It's a bunch of crap, you want to make the city better. Better for graft and kickbacks for you and your cronies is what you mean. You should talk about me and your mother, you phony bastard. Call me a pimp again, I'll bust your face . . ." Ben heard the phone slam down on the other end.

And on his end, he watched Nora's spirit slam down. She sank into a depression and became a recluse. Every morning she would call her son and get the same message from him, "Call me when you're married or you've dumped your pimp. And tell him to give your money back."

In his mind, Ben had dozens of arguments with Mason, all variations on why sin and social shame weren't the same; and why it was worse for Mason to be ashamed of his mother than angry at the society that penalized retired people; and did it occur to him that maybe God didn't see things the way he did; and on and on.

But instead of saying any of that to Mason, he retreated into his garden. Often he pleaded with Nora to join him there. She only wept and became morose. He offered to get married, but both of them knew they couldn't afford to do that. The bottom had fallen out of the housing market shortly after they'd bought the small house, and they were trapped.

Before he realized it, the garden was his world. Then it began to feel too important, to feel like work. He found himself worrying about it. At times he felt twinges of anger that others weren't working as hard as he was to cultivate gardens that would improve the neighborhood and make it more attractive, so maybe he could sell the house. And, while trying to be understanding, he resented Nora's deepening inaccessibility. Still, he couldn't leave her. The garden became small compensation, but all he had.

* * * * *

By late spring, it had become a ritual. Two nuns who taught at nearby St. John's school would come striding earnestly along the sidewalk, as if they hated exercising but were religiously determined to take what they called their "morning constitutional." It was hard for him to associate nuns with anything as physical as "a constitutional." It occurred to him one morning, watching them huff toward him, that they went about their walk as he had come to go about his gardening — as if it had to do with the serious improvement of something or other.

The first time they stopped, the shorter one introduced them both. "I'm Sister Cornelia," she said gasping, "and this is Sister Phoebe. We teach at St. John's."

The taller nun gushed about the beautiful flowers, saying the word "beautiful" with syrupy overtones that made him feel sticky. She went on to say how "sweet" it was of him to work so hard to make his place an "enclave of loveliness" and what a "noble and generous offering it was," though he noticed she gushed on without ever actually looking at anything in the garden, or at him.

He remembered reading in a newspaper once that the word "venom"and the word "Venus" come from the same root word, and that originally the words "poison" and "love potion" were interchangeable. Listening to Sister Phoebe, he could understand the connection.

That morning, and every morning after, Sister Phoebe would smile piously and say, " 'I planted, Apollos watered, but God gave the increase.' I'm sure you know that's from St. Paul, Mr. Gregory. And, of course, a man like you understands that all beauty and loveliness is from God. This garden is a testimony of faith, Mr. Gregory. I can see it."

One morning he actually asked her if all the aphids and cut worms and beetles were from God, too, but she just wagged a finger at him and smiled as though he were a piece of chocolate she coveted. He shrugged and let it go.

Sister Cornelia, on the other hand, never spoke of loveliness or beauty. There was wrath and judgment in her view of things. She always found something to complain about or to criticize: The garden was too small for so many flowers; he had the wrong species; the effect was confusion; he should simplify; he should organize it better; the colors of the different varieties clashed; he should get different kinds, more summer, fewer spring, no fall flowers because there was plenty of natural color in the fall and in the spring anyway. Once she suggested he add a small statue of the Virgin to the garden. "Of course, you are Catholic, aren't you?"

"No, I'm Zoroastrian," he answered in his most serious tone, "And polygamous and devoted to Zero Population Growth."

Sister Cornelia frowned and admonished, "You should never make light of serious matters. I know you are just joking, but it smacks of irreverence."

He smiled, "You're right, but I thought a little joke would be better than telling you I'm a direct descendent of Martin Luther and Katherine von Bora who, you know, was once a member of your very profession."

"Such impertinence," Sister Cornelia snorted.

Ben laughed, "Katherine's or mine?"

"Both," Sister Cornelia growled, stalking off, Sister Phoebe trailing her like a wolfhound on a leash.

But to her credit, Sister Cornelia remained undaunted and Sister Phoebe, her faithful companion. Every morning that it didn't rain, they'd meet him at the garden. But more often than he wished, he felt troubled by Sister Cornelia's criticism of his garden. Probably he had been presumptuous. Maybe he was wrong about it improving the neighborhood. Maybe it was all laughable. He thought about going to the garden club lectures to see how others did their gardens. Doubt and water began to pour over the plants at the same time.

* * * * *

One evening, after supper, Ben had just finished watering his plants when Alan Hicks came over from across the street. They'd talked only briefly in the few weeks they'd been neighbors, but Ben had sensed some tension.

"Workin' hard, I see," Hicks offered.

"Not really," Ben replied. "Like doing it."

"Yeah, guess you must, much time as you spend at it. Must be nice, bein' retired." There was an edge in Hick's voice.

"Some nice, some not so nice," Ben shrugged.

"Not havin' ta bust your chops for nobody must be nice. Got time for extra stuff, like this garden. One way for ya' ta keep tryin' ta please your woman, raisin' flowers at least."

Ben was wary, thinking Hicks was being provocative, making slurs about his manhood and Nora not being his wife. He wondered why people always exaggerated what they imagined was the worst about other people. Maybe it's envy, he thought, or maybe it gives them something delicious to talk about to spice up dull lives. He decided not to make an issue of it. "Yeah, but it tires me out, too. Matter-of-fact, it's about time for me to go in and sit down for a while before bed." He reached down to pick up his water bucket.

"Wait a minute, Gregory, before ya go. Me and some other guys in the neighborhood figured you might like to play a little poker with us this upcoming Friday night. We play every Friday night. Little recreation, ya know, among the guys."

Ben smiled at the invitation. It could be an honest effort to reach out to him or it could be a set-up. Or something in between. He chose to play it straight. "Thanks, Hicks. I'd like to, but I'm too poor for poker."

"Too poor? That some kinda put down of us who like playin' poker? What'aya gettin' at, Gregory?"

"Didn't mean it as a put down, Hicks. Not at all. I just mean I can't afford to lose. If you can't afford to lose, you don't play, right? That's one of the not so nice realities of retirement."

"Still sounds like a put down to me. Like the rest of us are scum for playin' poker for the few bucks we might lose just for the fun of playin'. You think you're too damn good for us, don't ya? That's really what you're sayin', ain't it?" Hicks just wasn't going to let it go. He'd come to unload and wasn't going to let up until he had.

Ben felt his bile rise. He spoke very deliberately. "No, Hicks, that's not what I'm saying. I'm saying I'm too poor. That's all."

"No, that ain't all, Gregory. You been actin' like you was better'n us since you moved here. Just remember, everybody's dirt's the same color."

Ben chuckled at Hick's nod to civility. "Dirt?" he replied. "You really talking about dirt or something else?" Now *he* was the one not letting it go.

"You know damn well what I'm talkin' about, Gregory. And yours is the same color as everybody elses', you air'gant bastard."

Ben couldn't help himself. "Really? I always wondered. I take it you've personally done a lot of research on the subject? Checked Omaha? Tucson? Miami? How about New Haven? Maybe Yalies' dirt is blue."

"You just provin' what I'm sayin', Gregory. Talkin' like I'm dumbass stupid and you're smarter'n and better'n me. Like puttin' in this garden, showin' us all up."

"Showing you up? Is that what this is all about, you coming over here tonight?" Ben thought he saw tears glistening in Hicks' eyes, but he couldn't be sure in the soft evening light.

"Damn sure. I should'a come before. Now all our women naggin' us to put one in. Like we don't work hard enough the way it is. Like our place ain't good enough the way it is. You're one conceited son-of-a-bitch is all I can say. Never bother'n to talk to none of us about nothin'. You c'n go straight to hell, far's I'm concerned." Hicks spun and walked away.

It was as if all Ben's frustration and perversity snapped out of control. A bumper sticker he'd seen flashed to mind, and the impulse was overwhelming. "Hey, Hicks," he yelled, "when your IQ hits thirty, sell." The curious pleasure he felt in his cruelty was almost immediately choked off by a surge of shame. There it was again, the feeling that haunted him. Was his shame a moral signal or just a crippling neurosis? After all, hadn't he put up with enough? Hadn't Hicks insulted him first? Why should he feel ashamed?

In any case, he didn't respond when Hicks turned and made an obscene gesture at him. He watched Hicks go, recalling how he had thought his garden would improve the neighborhood, excite others into following his lead, make the block more attractive to buyers, so he could get out. What was the whole thing about? Maybe he hadn't given Hicks a chance. Maybe the truth was somewhere between Hicks and him, between moral signal and emotional sickness.

That night he thought of calling Hicks and apologizing. Then he decided that might make Hicks feel cornered. The next morning, Ben sent Hicks a carefully worded postcard, but weeks went by without a response.

* * * * *

He might have given it up if it hadn't been for Buford Flynn. Buford was nine and in the third grade at St. John's. Every morning and every afternoon he walked past Ben's garden on the way to and from school, slowing down to watch whenever Ben was in his garden. Ben paid no attention. When, after several days, Buford ventured a timid "Hi," Ben responded with a gruff "Hello," neither wishing for nor inviting further talk.

Nevertheless, Buford adopted Ben. Ben wasn't good with kids, but Buford didn't notice. One day he stopped on the way to school and told Ben he lived alone with his grandmother "down that way," he said, pointing. Ben didn't ask for more information. Buford asked what kind of flowers the purple ones were, and Ben growled, "Hyacinth. Ask your teacher how to spell it. And you'd better not hang around here or you'll be late to school." Buford nodded and trudged off.

That afternoon he knocked on Ben's door and when Ben opened it, Buford said solemnly "H-y-a-c-i-n-t-h. Hyacinth. Can I have one for my Grandmother?"

Ben wanted to smile but somehow he felt embarrassed about it. So he just nodded and walked down the steps to pick a hyacinth for Buford. "Do you know Sister Cornelia?" he asked as he handed the flower to the little boy.

"Yep," Buford said, "she's the one taught me how to spell hyacinth."

"Oh," Ben responded, vaguely disappointed.

"She also told me hyacinths ain't too pretty 'cause they look sort of clobbered."

"You mean cluttered, don't you?" Ben asked.

"Yeah, maybe that's it. Don't matter, though. I think they're beautiful, and that's why I want one for my Grandmother. Sisters don't know everything."

Ben chuckled. "Better watch yourself, talking like that. I thought Catholic kids were taught to have respect for the Sisters."

"I'm only Catholic during the week," Buford confided. "Sundays I'm Baptist. Summers I'm Jewish. They got the best and cheapest summer camp. I gotta go now, or Grandmother will start worrying." He put out his little hand. Ben shook it. The friendship had begun.

It grew through the late spring and early summer. Almost every day Buford stopped to talk to Ben about things, from his Little League team to the best place to buy water ice, while asking about the different kinds of flowers and why Ben liked gardening and which ones were his favorites. Sometimes Ben let Buford water the plants or pull weeds or scratch the dirt loose around the roots. During those times they were quiet and serious as they concentrated on the work.

As the days grew hot and Ben's preoccupations with Nora and the neighborhood became more obsessive, Buford would ask Ben why he was feeling bad. Ben would get gruff then, and Buford would study him trying to figure out what he could say to make Ben feel better. When he couldn't think of anything, he'd go over and just touch Ben on the shoulder, wanting to hug him. Ben sensed Buford's care but felt shy in saying anything about his need or his gratitude for Buford's being there. After all, Ben was the man. So instead he'd snort, "You'd better get off to school," or "Your Grandmother's probably wondering where you are." Buford would simply nod and walk quietly away, not having the heart to tell Ben there wasn't any school in the summer and that his Grandmother knew exactly where he was.

When Buford went off to summer camp, Ben missed him intensely. Everything seemed to weigh heavily on him. Unexpectedly, he found himself ruminating about death, and it frightened him. At his age he'd thought he'd accepted death. He was surprised how much the thought of his nonexistence bothered him and set him to thinking about what life and death were really about. Maybe he was afraid of life as well as death. Or was angry at how similar they'd come to seem to him these days. He tried praying, but he wasn't sure what it was he was praying about. Was it his fear, or his anger, or just the damned, intractable fact of death — or his stupid inability to find his way out of any of it? His prayers droned from one subject to another but to no resolution. The only peaceful moments he had were the rare occasions when the simple beauty of one of his flowers absorbed his whole attention. Then he felt some quick, deep gratitude.

* * * * *

The dry August and hot early September turned into a wet autumn. The rain seemed to limit the number of times Buford and Ben had together. In his pride Ben wanted those times to seem entirely coincidental to Buford, and somehow to himself, so he made no pre-arrangements to see the boy.

One morning Buford decided his favorite flowers of all were the dahlias and the marigolds, ". . . 'cause," he said, "they sort of stay with you in your memory, you know, kind of like a promise when winter comes. What're your favorites, Ben?" he asked wide- eyed that snappy November morning as the gray clouds pulled up like a collar around the neck of the city and the feel of rain in the air made the last of the autumn leaves seem suddenly weary of their holding on.

"None," Ben growled. "None of them are my favorites." He wiped his nose with his finger. "None of 'em!" He wiped his nose again, then got out his handkerchief and blew his nose hard.

Buford went over and touched his shoulder. "I like 'em all, really," the boy said. "I ain't really got no favorites neither, Ben. It's just right now, I'm glad for the red and gold ones." He looked into Ben's face. "D-a-h-l-i-a," he spelled slowly, smiling, hoping to change something.

"Get to school," Ben said sternly, blowing his nose fiercely again. "And that isn't what I meant about none of them being my favorites. Oh, never mind. Get to school." The water in his eyes blurred his vision of Buford's yellow slicker going around the corner. "It's the cold wind," he mumbled to himself. As he opened the door, the dread came back. Nora waited like a lump in the overstuffed chair in the living room.

That morning, Nora's son was coming to help Ben take her to the psychiatric clinic at St. Monica's for tests. Her depression had gotten worse, she wasn't eating, wasn't talking, wasn't getting out of bed. "She's your mother," Ben had said insistently to Mason on the phone. "You ought to know I'm taking her to the hospital. She needs help. If word gets out she's your mother, that's just too bad. I can't protect you any longer."

There was a pause on the phone. "Okay, I'll go with you. We'll figure out something," Mason sighed.

It rained on the way to the hospital. Nora cried softly, apologizing for being "such a problem," until Ben wanted to tell her to "shut up," and then, ashamed that he felt so hostile toward her, put his arm around her and tried to reassure her. Nora would not be reassured.

When they got to the clinic, Mason registered Nora as his mother, gave his own address as his mother's, and introduced Ben as his mother's cousin. Ben shook his head at the lie but said nothing. All morning they waited restlessly in the lounge until a young resident introduced himself and told them that the initial tests indicated Nora should be admitted to the hospital until they could run more tests and get her properly medicated. Mason dealt with the admission procedures. A nurse with a ring of keys on her belt came and took Nora. As a cousin, at least Ben had visiting privileges.

In the late afternoon that day, the sun came out. Ben stood in the garden and watched for Buford, but he didn't come. That night the first frost arrived. Ben stepped outside before bed and watched his breath burst into little clouds. That made him feel lonely and fragile, as though each cloud were one less breath he had left. He went to bed and slept fitfully.

In the morning, by habit, he went to the garden. It was clear and cold. Shortly, Sister Cornelia and Sister Phoebe came striding down the street, leaving little breath clouds in their wake. "God still giving the increase, I see," gasped Sister Phoebe, "but soon winter will give the garden a season of rest."

"Your dahlias look awfully faded," observed Sister Cornelia. "No doubt you failed to feed them properly earlier."

"By the way," Sister Phoebe said, shifting to her most solemn tone, "have you heard that one of our students was struck by a car on the way home from school last evening?"

Ben froze.

"Yes, isn't it terrible? Car skidded on the wet leaves," Sister Cornelia went on. "Too bad, really. I wonder if the accident might have had anything to do with the fact that the boy insisted he was only a Catholic during the week . . ."

Ben grabbed her arm. "How is he? Is he alive?"

Sister Cornelia was unflustered. "Control yourself, Mr. Gregory, please. The boy is in Intensive Care at St. Monica's. He's expected to live, though he may not walk again, we're told."

Ben was shaking. "Buford Flynn? It's Buford Flynn?"

Sister Phoebe's sympathy was reflexive, "Oh, you knew Buford? Such a dear sweet, lovely boy. I'm sure the Almighty has some purpose in this, aren't you?"

"Oh my God, " Ben groaned.

* * * * *

He went into the house and cried. He began pounding on the table, the walls. That wasn't enough. He got his walking cane and charged through the door. The sight of the flowers enraged him. "You betrayed him," he screamed and started stomping on them. He cursed a steady stream, the least of the oaths being "damn." "Damn Mason," he stomped, "Damn Nora, damn the neighborhood, damn Sister Cornelia, Phoebe, Venus, Hicks, damn the whole god damn depressing thing."

He stomped and stomped and swung his cane wildly, at the flowers, the sky, the ground. Then he staggered off swinging at bushes, pigeons, anything; around the corner he stumbled, swinging toward St. John's school.

Rather than calming him or exhausting him, the rage and swinging built its own momentum and carried him into the church next to the school. The sun, rushing through the open door, then narrowing as the door closed, caught the silver spike on one hand of the crucifix over the altar and focused into a dazzling light that seemed to beckon Ben forward.

A single priest saying a mass in a small side chapel stopped in mid-phrase and watched incredulously as Ben climbed up on the main altar and yanked with all his strength at the nearly life-size crucifix. The cross holding the Christ figure came off in his arms, and they fell together on the huge altar. The priest remained frozen in disbelief and fear at the man's maniacal behavior, but he still heard Ben shriek with a strange, wild tenderness, "Good! Good! You've been up there long enough. You don't have to hurt any more."

Ben climbed off the altar and rushed up the aisle carrying the Christ figure over his shoulder. When he got outside, the sunlight dizzied him momentarily. He staggered drunkenly down the steps and started up the sidewalk. Shortly, he decided his load was too heavy. He spotted some bushes under a tree a few yards off the sidewalk, halfway between the church and the school yard. He put the crucifix down in the bushes and covered the Christ figure with leaves, like a blanket to warm him. Then Ben walked quickly to the bus stop and was the last passenger on the A bus that went to St. Monica's.

When the priest finally regained his senses, he ran to the rectory and called the police. The police didn't arrive in time to catch Ben.

Later that day, the social worker and the security guard reported back to the hospital that they had had no luck in finding leads to Ben Gregory's next of kin. An attorney from law firm representing the hospital finally called the police to report what had happened. The police investigation in the next few hours enabled them to put the pieces of the puzzle together, although they weren't sure what to do about it and told no one except the attorney from the law firm about it.

As night fell, and a full moon rose, Nora and Ben and Buford were all on different floors and in different units of St. Monica's, each fighting for life.

* * * * *

But the most incredible thing was that three of Buford's friends, on their way to school that morning, spied the Christ figure under the pile of leaves. Considering such a discovery an amazing, God-sent stroke-of-luck, and having a certain unquestioning faith in the efficacy of such charms as rabbit's feet, four-leaf clovers, and horse shoes, the three young boys considered this figure the biggest lucky charm that could possibly come anyone's way, and they decided to give it to the one who needed it most, namely their friend Buford, lying in St. Monica's hospital.

Whether it was circumstantial, or providential, it is nevertheless beyond explanation, and nearly beyond belief, that the three boys managed to spirit the Christ figure away before anyone saw them. Once launched on their good-will adventure, they spent most of the morning wrestling the Christ figure all the way to the hospital, up the stairs, past the guards and the nurses' stations, into Buford's little cubicle without being detected or stopped. Probably it actually happened because no one but the three boys believed it could happen. And maybe it had nothing to do with what happened afterward, but don't argue that with Ben or Buford, or Nora. They insist otherwise. As has been said, it is best to let mysteries sing their own songs.

Buford's first words after having been hit by the car were spoken to his three friends and the Christ figure. "Got him down, huh?" he whispered.

One of the boys answered, "Naw. We just found him and brought him here. Figured you could use good luck."

"Right," Buford smiled. "Leave him."

Because he asked, and because it did seem to help him, the authorities agreed to leave the Christ figure in Buford's cubicle, once they got over their initial embarrassment about how it got there. The newspapers and local TV carried the story, and Nora, who began responding to treatment and medication in the psychiatric ward, saw it on the evening news as a human interest story and recognized Buford. Then she overheard the nurses talking about the crazy man who had swatted the crucifixes off the hospital walls and then collapsed with a stroke. One of the nurses mentioned the man's name and said that nobody knew anything about him. Nora asked the nurse for more information, saying that he might be a friend of hers.

The total effect was like a shot of adrenalin to her. First she asked if she could visit Buford. It didn't take long for Nora and Buford to figure out together that Ben was the crucifix snatcher everyone was talking about, but they didn't tell anyone.

Then Nora simply asked for and received permission to visit Ben as well. Her visits were unsatisfactory, but Nora persisted. Ben remained critical and unconscious.

* * * * *

With the resiliency of youth, Buford quickly progressed out of the critical stage and, though his legs remained paralyzed, he managed to badger his doctor into letting the attendants wheel him down to visit Ben every day. A week went by, and Ben remained in a coma. Finally, Buford went around and got flowers from all the people he could beg or borrow them from and took all the arrangements with him to visit Ben. And he talked the attendant into bringing the the Christ figure with them, since he decided maybe Ben needed the luck even more than he did. He got the attendant to prop the Christ figure against the wall at the foot of Ben's bed and put flowers every place else. When everything was in place around Ben's bed and the machines, Buford leaned over and whispered in Ben's ear: "H-y-a-c-i-n-t-h, hyacinth," over and over again. For four days this went on.

Finally, Ben responded. Slowly he opened one eye and, though he was very hesitant in his speech, he spoke those five words to Buford more clearly than he would speak again for months: "Aren't you late for school?"

* * * * *

Now it is May again. The way back has been slow and painful for each of them, and each of them bears the scars of their struggle. Buford walks with crutches. Ben's left leg and arm are weak, his speech still slow, slurred, and frustrating to him, his smile crooked on one side. He needs his cane to walk. Tears still come easily to Nora, but the smiles are more frequent, as are the curses. She fights now, however timidly, even with Ben.

And she goes regularly to visit her son and daughter-in-law and grandson, riding the bus and arriving unannounced at their door. They greet her with a shrug and let her in, for fear she'll make a scene if they don't, which she would. Actually, it seems to matter less to them since Mason lost his election, which he seems almost relieved about. In fact, sometimes the shrug of greeting is followed by a brief hug, and occasionally Mason and family are seen at Nora and Ben's house. So they are all adjusting. Some might even say flourishing. Sister Phoebe would, which is . . . enough.

Ben and Buford go to physical therapy three times a week together. But the therapy isn't the hardest part for Ben. The hardest thing is coming to terms with some things about himself. It would have been easy to elicit sympathy, to become a victim, to explain what happened to him by blaming it on others, on the circumstances of his situation. To help him prove his case, had he wanted to try that, he had a list of charges and offenders and the evidence of a piece of earth stomped into a hardness no one could believe ever was a garden. But shame kept him from it. Besides, it was a garden, even if he'd mostly lost track of the pleasure of it when he turned it into work.

During those long days and nights in the hospital, studying that Christ figure propped in the corner, he had realized something. He had tried to tell Nora what it was. At first he attempted to speak, in halting, stroke-impoverished words: "I been . . . w'ike . . . seed . . . tha' wou'dn' . . . w'et . . . se'wf . . . be pwo'anted . . ." Then, in frustration, he motioned for a pencil and paper. All of a sudden it seemed terribly urgent to make her understand, to understand it for himself.

I been like seed. Refused be planted, grow. Lost trust. Not trust anything after while. Defended all time. Got ashamed at wrong things. Lost myself. We lost ourselves. What we afraid of? God, no more fear, please. No more! Say "damn." Say "love you!" Trust! Take chance. Like Buford.

It was agonizing to watch him struggle for words, but afterward there was an ease about him.

Anyway, it's May again. And most mornings, if you're in the neighborhood before they go to therapy, you can see a little boy on crutches and an old man with a cane and watering can — and a woman with wonderful crows feet around her eyes, like furrows in a cornfield — all working away on a little garden in front of a row house around the corner and about a block down from St. John's school.

Some days, if you catch the time right, you might see a tall nun down on her knees next to Buford, watering one of the plants and actually getting her hands dirty in what she still insists on calling, "the lovely, sweet earth," while another nun and the old man yell at each other until they start to laugh.

And on a Saturday, you'll see maybe one or two other guys working on similar little gardens in front of other houses on the block. You'll even notice the one named Alan Hicks coming over to talk to the old man and getting advice from him every little while. The only advice the old man gives him, though, is a shrug and a pat on the back.

But the most curious thing about the little garden in front of the row house around the corner from St. John's school is that somehow, propped up in one corner of it, as though lying on its back, knees raised and ankles crossed in a relaxed, peaceful manner, arms stretched out and hands seeming to caress the flowers, is the Christ figure that once hung over the altar of the church next to the school. It was put there by diocesan permission, at the stubborn insistence of Sister Cornelia and her order, after it had been desacralized by the fairly willing pastor in charge at St. John's. It is amazing how well the figure seems to fit in the surroundings, and sometimes, when the sun slants a certain way, there are those who swear you can see a smile on the face of the Christ.

It's Ben's garden, on the little patch between house and street in a struggling but strangely appealing city neighborhood. He even smiles crookedly and nods when the tall nun reminds him, needlessly, each morning, dirt smudging her face, "I planted, Apollos watered, but God gave the increase." But then he adds, "Some increase!" after which his crooked smile turns into a giggling, slightly drooling, quite unself-conscious laugh. His heart is really in it, at last!

A kind of communion taking

O God,
>   I cannot grasp you
>>   or escape you,
>   but would stand
>>   this twilight watch
>>>   with you,
>>   this end of day aware,
>>   this resurrection glance.

Sunlight smears its seal
>   upon the shadowed earth,
>>   a crimson, purple promise
>>>   that darkness won't prevail;
>   bird song drips a weary vespers,
>>   Venus dons her radiant veil,
>>>   crickets raise their prayers;
>   a small child nods to storied sleep,
>>   traffic hums toward home somewhere,
>>>   an old man walks his faithful dog;
>   kids play stickball by the street light,
>>   while a little wheelchaired-sister
>>>   swears encouragement at them
>>>>   and plays battery-powered rap.

Leaning on elbows around dinner tables,
>   people sip and talk, sometimes touch,
>>   a kind of communion taking
>>>   while the dishes wait,
>>>>   and the bad news we pay for
>>>>>   flickers on the television.

Out back is a rose nodding white,
>   the faint smell of sweet basil,
>>   a beaded necklace of impatiens
>>>   fringing an audacious plot of weeds;

and across the way, a precious moment
    steals through an unguarded window
        as two wonderfully oblivious lovers
            kiss, caress themselves to sighs,
                and me to a blushing smile,
reminding me I've heard faith is a blush
    in your presence.

O God,
    where have I been?
        I've heard and seen this all before,
            these small and tender mercies,
        but realized not the miracle,
            acknowledged not the gift,
        took not the nourishment,
            received not the grace,
        ignored incarnation,
            forgot what it is you love.

O God,
    awe is where the healing is,
        and the soar of confidence.
    Gratitude coalesces me
        into some integrity,
            some merge
                of trustworthiness,
                of love,
                    of reverent resolve
    to celebrate this life, this earth,
    to brave a just and joyful work
    and a more adoring watch with you,
        sailing this cosmic Tiberian Sea
            on this fishing boat of earth
                toward resurrection breakfasts
                on near, far distant shores.

THE UNEXPLAINABLE

Resonant assurance

O God
    of unfathomable depths
        and unapproachable heights,
    since it is through mystery
        that you come closest to me,
    and through awe
        that I come closest to you,
    grant me
        the integrity
            to be tutored by the questions
                awe eddies up in me,
                    but pride stanches down;
        the courage
            to venture beyond the answers
                fear bids me make
                    absolute and inviolable;
        the wisdom
            to respect the difference
                arrogance erases between
                    the yet unknown, the always unknowable;
        the confidence
            to love boldly and inclusively
                amidst the uncertainties
                    tyranny and timidity reduce to creeds;
        the trust
            to rest in the resonant assurance
                that what I really need in this life
                    comes not only by dependable design,
            but in strange, unexplainable deviations —
                haunt of burning bushes,
                    untamed prophets —
            because you are always going about your
                gracious,
                    unpredictable,
                      ingenious
                        creating.

So, O wondrous God,
　　　in awe,
　　　　　not desperation or resignation,
　　I pray for those I carry in my heart
　　　　whose lives have flattened
　　　　　　into a sentence of single dimension,
　　　　　　　a certain, inevitable boredom,
　　　　　　　　　loneliness,
　　　　　　　　　anxiety,
　　　　　　　　　sorrow,
　　　　　　　　　despair,
　　　　　　　　　sickness,
　　　　　　　　　guilt,
　　　　　　　　　hopelessness,
　　　　　　　　　endings,
　　　that in some way,
　　　　　past their understanding or mine,
　　　　　　past the limits of the world and time,
　　you are even now working in them,
　　　　with them,
　　　　　　for them,
　　　　　　　as in, with, for me,
　a different,
　　　liberating,
　　　　　saving,
　　　　　　altogether amazing,
　　　　　　　baby eyes,
　　　　　　　　desert dawn,
　　　　　　　　　misty moon,
　　　　　　　　　　sea-storm,
　　　　　　　　　　　kingdom come,
　　　　　　　　　　　　awesome thing.

Humbled by the strangeness

O Holy One,
    after twilight's soft consolation
        I tremble when night rubs softly on the window
            as an even softer warning
                of how thin is the layer of what we know,
                how thick the overlay of proud assumption —
                    making the darkness your gift,
                    the tremor, my heart's praise.
        I recall a mid-day voice
            coming from me but somehow not my own,
            shocking me to gagging awareness
                of what cannot be bought or sold,
                but only betrayed by vain pretension —
                    making the shock your judgment,
                    the gag, my soul's confession.

I pause now,
    humbled by the strangeness of things,
    quieted by the fragile, preciousness of life,
    heartened by the incomprehensible greatness of you,
    drawn into that galvanic space between us,
        that wilderness of curious, childlike clarity
            of living shadows,
                fluttering wings,
                    tiptoeing winds,
                        dancing memories,
                          flickering possibilities,
                            endless connections,
                              my own breathing,

where I can shed, scatter
the smoldering angers and resentments,
the cruelty of withheld words,
the danger of unquestioned roles,
the arrogance of unexamined blaming
that shrivels me
and by which I shrivel others.

I pause now,
intrigued by what I've ignored,
released by my great need of you
more urgent than my strutting doubts,
my puffed up demands for proof,
my inane claims to know your mind
when I don't even know my own,
and fear to know it better,
to ask you to take me, go with me
to some uncharted space inside out
where I will hear music not my own,
a rustling in the air;
see a pulse of flame,
a parting of the clouds;
smell the musk of fertile earth,
the astringent incense of my soul;
and realize, in a stitch of healing,
how petty, sad, unnecessary
are my cleverness, deceits, anxieties,
resentments, greeds, lusts, ambitions,
how vast the realms of grace.

I pause now,
       summoned by my essential loneliness,
              the burden and splendor of freedom,
       to stretch toward your presence;
       to embrace these contradictions that I am
              of wildness and tenderness,
              fallenness and faithfulness,
              blindness and farsightedness;
       and to love myself entire
              as I would love my neighbor;
       to wrestle the torments and tensions of my life,
              the demons and angels, hungers and kingdoms,
                     into some dim light of dawn,
                            some poetic blessing,
                                   some priestly scream or prayer,
                                          some prophetic limp of creativity,
                                   some honest word,
                                          some honest being,
              nothing fully explained,
                     but fully ventured,
       into a letting go of what success hangs on to,
              a leaving of where caution hunkers down,
       a going on into the unknown,
              inside out, outside in, yet deep between us,
       into that strange promised place
              of forgive, just, trust, love,
                     and possible;
       into that mysterious promised time
              of praise, peace, hope, joy —
                     fulfilled.

D-d-do ya s-s-see 'im?

O God,
    your touch is light,
        for sometimes, maybe more,
            you wrap grace in laughter,
        or perhaps laughing
            just puts me lightly in touch with
                what I've taken massively for granted;
    often it seems your witness is a clown,
        or close to one,
            or perhaps closer to something
                even more incongruous:
                    a walleyed seer,
                    a prophet with a stutter,
                    an angel in disguise.

"D-d-do ya s-s-see 'im?"
    I was standing on the corner
        waiting for a traffic light,
            or maybe for a visitation.
    A man, obviously homeless,
        rose up from the grate
        ski-capped, sneakered, whiskered,
        layered with sweaters, grime,
            shopping bag in one hand,
                the other pointing
                    first at me,
                    then at some distant scene
                    his walleye seemed to spot.

"D-d-do ya s-s-see 'im?"
    O God, I laughed,
        first to scoff,
            needing to prove my sophistication
                to the others waiting for the light,
        then in embarrassment
            that he'd chosen me for this exchange,
                his pointing hand now tugging on my arm,
        finally in some confusion
            over what I say I believe, O God,
                and the discomfort I was feeling.

"D-d-do ya s-s-see 'im?"
  Red turned green, the others went on,
    I stayed unsure why except, I suppose,
      the light changed differently for me;
  and I laughed again,
    in grudging respect for his insistence,
      in some small delight for this diversion
       on a dull, down day,
      a bit of relief that for a moment
       I'd broken stride.
Honestly, I thought of you, fleetingly,
    as if you'd be proud of me for this,
  and in that double think, nearly lost the gift,
    save for his tug, his walleyed gaze at me,
      his nothing more important question.

"D-d-do ya s-s-see 'im?" He pointed urgently.
  It's J-j-jesus, a-a-ain't it?"

This time I laughed
  as at a child's wonderment over some magic
    long lost in adult explanations, skepticisms,
      there being in me a sudden spark of love
       for this stuttering, walleyed seer
        who alternated between tugging and pointing.
I looked and saw
  a woman limping wearily up the street,
    grocery bag in one arm, child in the other;
  teen-agers arm in arm,
    full of dreams, music, hormones;
  a school bus, like Noah's ark,
    bearing its precious cargo home;
  traffic honking up the avenue
    purging the day's frustrations;
  human beings going to and fro
    in the streets on all their human errands,
      hoping to find what they're looking for,
       like me, like this man beside me, pointing.
I looked at him.

O God,
    this time, he was laughing.
    "T-t-told ya s-s-so. It's J-j-jesus, r-r-right?
        I k-k-knew ya'd s-s-see 'im. G-g-glad, a-a-ain't ya?
    He's g-g-glad, M-m-molly."
        He called to a friend I hadn't noticed,
            leaning against a building at our back.
    He laughed, like a child verified, affirmed.
        Was that a wishfulness only,
            an illusion, or was it real?
    All I know is that verifying
        was more than I had done,
            but somehow I felt it, too,
                and laughed with him,
                    then took his hand in mine
                        and gave him all the cash I had.
    "T-t-thanks, b-b-brother," he said,
        his walleye looking at me, I think,
            but more, beyond me to what he'd pointed to,
            and I had seen at his insistence.

O God,
    do such seers see what isn't there,
        or do I not see what is?
    Or is it that mostly I do not know
        what it is I see?
Grace, O God,
    grace to see with more than eyes,
        grace to feel the tug,
            heed the stammer.
    "It's J-j-jesus, r-r-right?
        G-g-glad, a-a-ain't ya?"
            Yes. Yes.
I thank you, brother.
    O God, I thank you,
        thank you,
            thank you, God.

This catch of light

Eternal One,
    what unutterable beauty
        is laced into this world:
late afternoon after rain clouds
    hang in pink-edged, purple ruffles
        over the green-gray ocean;
  a congregation of birds
    brown as sand, swift as shivers,
        wheel as one at some primordial signal,
        pivot against the dark clouds,
        catch the light on white breasts,
          a flash of inspiration,
          a quick revelation
            that takes my breath away,
            returns it in deep inhalation.
O God,
  I say in spontaneous acknowledgment,
    as honest a prayer as I can utter.

Now, more reflectively,
  I ponder before still O-God-you:
    the pivot of the birds
      was perhaps nothing to them
      but the way of the hunt,
        an instinct, a mere exercise,
        the sight of prey, a scent of danger;
    but to me their ballet
      was an abrupt disclosure
      of some incredible intention
        beyond their power to define or mine to ignore,
        our being creatures together.
  Together's the revelation,
    isn't it, O God?
  Beauty being not just in wing
    or breast, or burst of light,
      nor in my beholding eye,
        or breath, or brain,

but in the meeting,
　　　the curious, mysterious between,
　　　　　　the surprise of connection
　　　　　　　　　we were imaged for from the beginning,
　　creation becoming conscious of itself, of me,
　　　　　and me of you,
　　　　　　　　in something like this strange surge
　　　　　　　　　　of wing and wonder,
　　　　　　　　　　　　and then the longing.

O God,
　　　I say again because I'm caught
　　　　　(if but for this fraction,
　　　　　　　become the measure of my life)
　　　　　　　　　in this catch of light,
　　　　　　　　　　　this feathered wheel,
　　　　　　　　　　　　　this flash of revelation,
　　and I glimpse an essential weave of grace:
　　　　salvation is communal,
　　　　　　　the ours
　　　　　　　　　of beauty, truth, hope,
　　　　　　　the we
　　　　　　　　　of mercy, wholeness, atonement,
　　　　　　　the together
　　　　　　　　　of wolves and lambs and all reunion,
　　　　　　　the us
　　　　　　　　　of wedding feasts, Samaritans, prodigals
　　　　　　　　　　　and every occasion of rejoicing;
　　　　　　the love that is, and never ends, being relational,
　　　　　　　the meeting,
　　　　　　　　　the surprise of connection
　　　　　　　　　　　you imaged for this we of me
　　　　　　　　　　　　　from the beginning of the any.
　　So I am less than me
　　　　without the others,
　　　　　　and this us is lesser still
　　　　　　　without the you
　　　　　　　　　who are our all.

SAM WHO-AM AND MURPH

Everything about Murph's Tavern is run down, including Murph. It has taken fifty-two years of Murph's proprietorship to get that way. Outside hangs a faded green sign that announces the owner's name without the aid of the neon, which had long since stopped working.

Inside, the tavern is small, cluttered with boxes of empty bottles, permeated by the smell of stale beer and the accumulated layer of grease around the small grill in a corner behind the bar. Next to the grill is a refrigerator in which, alongside the cheese and hamburger, Murph keeps a supply of chocolate-covered peanut clusters he munches while cooking, talking to the trade, and instructing his willing but plodding helper.

Tucked, taped, pinned in every available cranny of the bar are faded newspaper clippings, curled black-and-white as well as color photographs, dusty medals and trophies, campaign buttons, slogans on cups, plaques, torn samplers — the historic trail of Murph's fifty-two years on that corner.

If you ask him about that history, Murph shrugs and says, "Yeah, I seen lots a changes while I'm here, most of 'em not so good. I tell ya somethin'. I close at nine every night. People say I'm dumb. They ask, 'What kinda tavern closes at nine? How ya make money like that?' Know what I say? I say if any funny stuff goes on out there, muggings, drugs, stuff like that, I'm already outta here. Money ain't everything. Tell ya somethin' else. Some guy I know comes in here blowin' his money and neglectin' his family, I tell 'im ta get outta here, go home. Troubles, like one of them viruses, spreads around easy if ya ain't careful. Don't need no more trouble, me or the world. So ya gotta take precautions, ya know, while ya can. But I ain't got long here anyhow. Whatta ya gonna do?" Then he pops a peanut cluster in his mouth as if the candy were a question mark, or maybe an exclamation point.

Murph looks like a disheveled owl. His chubby body sags over short legs. His dark eyes dominate his large round face and peer out through black, horn-rimmed glasses. What hair he has is almost white. His clothes are frayed, spotted, made up of odd matches of stripes and plaids, coats from one old suit, pants from another, never anything new, as if the point of dressing for him is to cover the body, keep warm, and use up all his clothes before he dies.

His stories are honed and polished, word for word the same every time he tells them. "I'm Irish, ya know," he'll say absently while frying a hamburger. "Murph is short for Patrick John Ezekiel Murphy. Ya wanna know why 'Ezekiel,' which ain't exactly no Irish name? I'll tell ya. My people come over from Ireland, no question about it, but the family secret was that somewhere way back some Jewish blood snuck in on account of a crazy ancestor from near Cork gettin' drunk and signin' on for the crusades and bringin' back a Jewish wife who was pregnant and looked Irish, or somethin' like that.

"My mother, God rest her soul, didn't think that was nothin' ta be ashamed of, but it took her six kids ta persuade my old man ta give one of us a Jewish name t'honor that grand old ancestor on her side. Sad, peoples' pinched ways of lookin' at one another, ain't it? Anyway, when I come along, number seven, I got it, the Jewish name. Ezekiel. Patrick John Ezekiel. Priest almost wouldn't baptize me. Took an extra buck in the box from my old man — which was a lot in those days — plus the priest not havin' ta say Ezekiel, only mouth it, when he baptized me, ta get the job done. But him not sayin' it don't change it. My mother give it ta me and that's my name. Whatta ya gonna do?" By the end of the story the hamburger is burning and the smoke stings your eyes.

There's room for only twelve, fifteen stools on the customers' side of the bar. There are seldom that many people in the place except at midday when Murph gives free lunches to homeless people. Murph's Tavern is in a once fine, upper-middle class section of the city that for thirty years has experienced urban decay, racial change, and a bad reputation. Houses deteriorated and businesses fled. Recently, there has been an upturn in the area, and real estate speculators are buying and fixing up property all around.

However, that upturn has not changed the situation for street people. So every day, from mid-morning to mid-afternoon, Murph passes out food to his flock of homeless. It is rumored that several homeless actually live in the run down rooms over Murph's Tavern. And that's where this story really begins.

One of the real estate speculators made Murph an offer for the tavern, intending to make it an up-scale cocktail lounge. Murph turned the offer down cold.

"What'm I gonna do if I don't have this place?" Murph inquired when the speculator made his offer. "Sit in the park and drool? It ain't the money. Here, I belong. They'll have ta carry me out. No thanks. I ain't sellin'. Now ya gotta 'xcuse me. I hav'ta serve lunch ta my friends."

The speculator looked around. "Where? Upstairs?" he asked.

Murph smiled, "No. Too old ta climb stairs much anymore. Right here."

"You serve lunch to friends in a dump . . . place like this?" the speculator sniffed.

"Well, they ain't exactly just friends. You could say they're people who don't live around here." Murph smiled as he moved away. "They don't mind a dump like this. Whatta ya gonna do?"

The speculator apologized, "I'm sorry. I didn't mean to offend."

Murph turned back, deadpan. "Not while you're tryin' ta buy my property anyway, right? 'xcuse me, I really gotta work now."

It was the speculator who reported Murph's Tavern to the City Health Department for unsanitary food preparation, and to the Bureau of Licenses and Inspection to investigate whether people were being illegally housed on the second floor of the tavern. The speculator thought the aggravation might force Murph to reconsider selling.

But strangely enough, not only did the Health Department and L&I investigators visit Murph's Tavern, but so did media people. No one was sure how the press found out about Murph, or how Channel 6 happened to send a crew out to interview him, but suddenly Murph was on the evening news, and stories about him were in all the papers. His celebrity status embarrassed him.

The five o'clock TV live coverage panned the neighborhood, then showed Murph passing out food to his friends. The interviewer asked Murph how long he'd been feeding the homeless in his tavern.

Murph answered, "Maybe five or six years, give or take a couple of days."

The interviewer laughed. "And what made you start doing it?"

"Somethin' just come over me one day. Like someone tapped me on the noggin' and just put the idea in there," Murph said. "It's a free country, ain't it? Whatta ya gonna do?"

The interviewer nodded. "But a lot of people don't help like this," she replied, pointing to the homeless people eating at the bar.

"I don't care what other people do. People're always comin' in and havin' a beer and talkin' about big stuff, like how t'run the government or solve some crisis or other. Everybody's brilliant. I use t'get off on that stuff myself 'til I realized it was useless. This here I do. 'Cause I can, is why. It's real, like. But it ain't no big deal."

The interviewer smiled. "Murph," she said, "I'll wager Channel 6 viewers *will* think it's a big deal. It takes a good man to use his own money and his own business to feed homeless people. You're to be congratulated. You're an example for the rest of us. Wouldn't you agree, Jack? Now back to you in the studio. This is Deborah Alcorn for . . ."

Murph interrupted and pulled the microphone toward him. "Wait a minute. I ain't doin' this 'cause I'm good. It's more 'cause if ya ain't careful, the bad stuff in ya sort of takes over. Whatta ya gonna do? Listen! I ain't no better'n these people. None a you is, really, either. Ya gonna get it all wrong makin' me out ta be some kinda hero or somethin'. I ain't even religious anymore. I used ta be Catholic, being Irish and all, but . . ."

The TV station cut Murph off, and the crew on scene moved in to calm Murph down and get the microphone away from him. On the six and eleven o'clock news, Murph's outburst was edited out, but it was too late. Reports of the interview spread. Murph was an instant folk hero.

The flood of publicity had three results: One was that L&I and the Health Department suspended their investigation of Murph's Tavern for fear it would provoke bad press; two, Murph vowed he would never again allow TV stations or newspaper reporters in his tavern or near his person; three, Murph got several more offers for his property, all of which he refused.

One other thing happened at the same time that may or may not have been the result of Murph's publicity. New faces appeared among the homeless at lunch time. Murph talked to each about their circumstances, and while he tried to discourage some, he never actually turned any away. Within a month things had returned to what seemed normal to Murph, though his meager savings were shrinking under the burden of having to buy more food.

Then the angel appeared. It happened like this. One noon about three weeks after Easter, a new person showed up in the soup line. The person wore a heavy coat under which was a bulky sweater under which was a plaid dress under which were jogging pants. On one foot was a rubber boot, on the other a hightop sneaker. A ski cap was pulled down over a bushy head of hair, and over the ski cap was tied the sort of straw hat women often wear while gardening. On one hand there was a glove, on the other a mitten, and in both were shopping bags.

The new person went to the far end of the bar and sat on the floor, back against the wall. After lunch Murph leaned over, hands on his knees, and began to talk to the new person who was slurping the last bit of soup from a plastic bowl.

"What's your name?" he asked.

"Sam Who-Am," was the answer.

Murph looked puzzled. "Sam, huh? Funny name for a woman, ain't it?"

"Who said I'm a woman?" Sam Who-Am retorted.

"Nobody. I just figured ya was, with the woman's coat and the dress and the long hair. So I was wrong. So okay, Sam, you're a man."

Sam Who-Am's head cocked to one side. "Who said I was a man?"

Murph frowned. "You did."

Sam Who-Am looked Murph in the eye. "No, I didn't."

Murph was struck by the clarity of Sam Who-Am's eyes. The eyes looked very young for such an old face. "Yeah, I guess ya didn't actually say that. So ya are a woman after all."

"No, I didn't say that either," Sam Who-Am insisted, continuing to gaze into Murph's now befuddled face.

Murph straightened up. "Enough with the games, Sam. Which are ya, a man or a woman? Ya gotta be one or the other."

The corners of Sam Who-Am's mouth turned up slightly. "Who said I gotta be one or the other?"

"Who said?" Murph answered incredulously. "Mother Nature! God! That's who said. You gotta be one or the other, unless you're one a them circus freaks what claims ta be both, and I don't believe that stuff anyway."

Sam Who-Am smiled more broadly, and Murph noticed that the teeth seemed very white for an old street person, even though one was missing in front. "No, I'm not that kind of freak, Murph."

"So which are you?" Murph asked again, trying to control his exasperation, "a man or a woman."

"Sit here and I'll tell you," Sam Who-Am replied, patting an empty spot on the floor. Murph nodded his head wearily and sat.

"I'm a burning bush," Sam Who-Am said when Murph had settled in.

Murph shook his head. "Why do I get all the nut cases?" he muttered. Then he added, "I have ta admit ya do smell a little like somethin' burnin' though."

"I'm a burning bush," Sam Who-Am insisted, "a messenger from God."

"As long as ya ain't from L&I or the Health Department," Murph shrugged.

"It's true," Sam Who-Am insisted, softly. "I am really an angel."

"Oh yeah, of course. And I'm the Pope. What hospital ya been in?" Murph wheezed, struggling to get to his feet.

Sam Who-Am put a hand on Murph's arm. "No hospital, Murph."

Murph gave up the attempt to get up. He was too tired. He realized he'd been feeling very tired lately. "Okay, no hospital. But ya ain't from around here. Where're ya from?"

Sam Who-Am smiled again, "I've been around here many times. You just didn't notice. But I am from other places, too."

Murph sighed. "Like China? Or Korea, maybe?"

It was Sam Who-Am's turn to look puzzled. "China? Why do you say that?"

Murph pinched his nose, blew, and then let the air out in a rush. "Because your other name sounded Oriental or somethin'. What was it again?"

"Oh, you mean, 'Who-Am'?"

"Yeah. Sounds Oriental. But ya don't look like that, no slant eyes or nothing."

"I'm not Oriental," Sam Who-Am chuckled.

"Then what?" Murph pressed. "Armenian? Eye-ranian maybe? What's 'Who-Am'?"

"It's a long story," Sam Who-Am said.

Murph nodded. "I'll just bet it is. Look, I like ta know who I'm feedin' here. So tell me the shortest, straightest way ya can."

Sam Who-Am rubbed those young eyes. "You know who Moses is, right?"

Murph put his head back against the wall. "Yeah, I know. Everyone knows that. Besides, I got a little Jewish in me from way back. Ninety-nine percent Irish, though."

Sam Who-Am continued. "Remember when God told Moses to go lead his people out of Egypt, and Moses said no one would follow him? And God said, 'Just tell them I sent you.' And Moses said, 'How will they know who you are? What's your name?' And God said, 'My name is I am who I am.' Only, the burning bush where God's voice was coming from coughed and made a crackling sound right at that moment, and Moses thought God said, 'My name is Sam Who-Am.'

"That misunderstanding caused a lot of problems. When Moses got to Egypt and told the Pharaoh to let his people go because the God whose name was Sam Who-Am said so, the Pharaoh laughed at him. Same thing happened when Moses told the Jews. Nobody had ever heard of a God named Sam Who-Am. Took all those plagues to straighten Pharaoh out about it, and forty years in the wilderness to get the Jews shaped up after that." Sam Who-Am was laughing now.

Murph couldn't help smiling. "What nut-house hospital did ya say ya were in?" he asked. "That's the craziest thing I ever heard. You shouldn't joke about stuff what's in the Bible."

Sam Who-Am touched Murph's arm. "It really isn't entirely a joke, Murph. Among angels, Sam Who-Am is the code name for things people don't understand — or can't quite believe. Like angels. Like me."

Murph studied Sam Who-Am for a moment. Then very quietly he said, "Sam Who-Am, huh? All right. It ain't a bad name 'cause I sure don't understand ya comin' in here like this, those young eyes lookin' out of that old face, teeth all straight 'cept one missin' and none of 'em havin' no stains on 'em or nothin'. Somethin' funny about ya, all right."

Sam Who-Am's hand covered the mouth. "I guess I didn't get all the bugs out of my impersonation."

Murph smiled. "Ya got quite an imagination, I'll give ya that. Must a kissed the Blarney stone sometime in your life. I don't buy ya being no angel, but ya can eat here when ya want. What else can I say? Whatta ya gonna do?" He started to get up again, but this time felt a bit dizzy. "Guess I'll just sit here a while longer," he said, sliding back to his seat beside Sam Who-Am.

After a moment Sam Who-Am said, "You don't go to church anymore. Why not?"

Murph looked at Sam Who-Am. "How'd ya know that? Was ya around when that TV bunch was here, and I told 'em somethin' about that? Is that how ya knew?"

"Let's just say I knew," Sam Who-Am replied. "So, why don't you go anymore?"

"I ain't sure," Murph sighed. "I guess it was that the confessions took too long."

"Took too long?" Sam Who-Am asked. "What do you mean?"

"Just that," Murph said. "I used ta go in and try ta tell the priest all the stuff that's wrong inside me and all the stuff I done and said that ain't right or true for just one lousy day, and it took such a long time I couldn't never finish, even one day's worth, let alone a whole week between masses. Other people didn't seem ta have no trouble, but I did. So I felt there was somethin' really wrong with me. Like I didn't belong. Didn't deserve ta belong. So I stopped goin'. That's all. Whatta ya gonna do?"

Sam Who-Am touched Murph's cheek. "Is that really all, Murph?"

Tears filled Murph's eyes and trickled down his cheeks. "I don't guess it is," he whispered hoarsely. "It's lonely not belongin'. I act like it ain't, but it is. I think maybe that's got somethin' ta do with my feeding homeless people in here. It's like for a hour or so we all belong. For a little while we ain't none of us homeless. Only I ain't never able ta say nothin' about it ta none of 'em ta help make it real for us. Whatta ya gonna do?"

"You're talking to me," Sam Who-Am reminded him.

"I was just thinkin' that same thing," Murph said, taking off his glasses and wiping his eyes with the back of his chubby hands. "It's a wonder, ain't it?"

They sat quietly for a moment, and then Murph went on. "Sometimes early in the morning, or at night when there ain't nobody there, I go sit in Saint Madeleine's and think what it would be like ta be there, me and all these people here together in that beautiful place. I sit there thinkin' if that could happen, then there wouldn't be no more vacancies in peoples' eyes or lives . . . or whatever.

"Wouldn't it be somethin' if that could happen? But that place and this one's like two different worlds that can't get together. Be somethin', wouldn't it, ta get 'em together? Only, lately I been thinking it ain't just two worlds. It's really like two parts a me can't get together. So I sit there wonderin' why I'm so lonely, why I'm feelin' so empty? I don't know. Sam Who-Am's a good name for God if it's like ya say, the name of things people don't understand. Whatta ya gonna do?"

Sam Who-Am leaned forward to engage Murph's eyes. "Murph, those world's aren't so far apart. There are angels in all of them. Really! When you go to Saint Madeleine's, sometimes you talk to a Sister there, don't you?"

Murph frowned. "How'd ya know that? Are ya from Saint Madeleine's? Are ya a Sister in disguise? Is that who ya are?"

Sam Who-Am's hands went up in denial. "No, no. I told you who I am, Murph. Heaven is not far from earth either, even if you can't believe that. I just know that Sister Mary Martha prays for you."

Murph shrugged. "Maybe she does. I ain't gonna ask how ya know that, or her name. It's for sure I don't understand ya, Sam. The Sister said she'd pray for me, and I don't figure she'd lie. But so what? What good're her prayers ta me?"

Sam Who-Am spoke as to a child. "Murph, what good is your feeding the homeless to Sister Mary Martha?"

"I never thought about it," Murph answered after a long pause. "Maybe if one of these here people's her brother or sister, it'd be good for her."

Sam Who-Am clapped. "That's it, Murph! You saw it."

Murph was puzzled. "Saw what?"

Sam Who-Am answered enthusiastically, "Saw what most people don't see. We do belong to each other; heaven and earth belong to each other. We're connected by bread and prayers and everything else. Sam Who-Ams are about helping people find that out, see that. You see it, Murph."

"I do?" Murph replied.

"Of course," Sam Who-Am insisted. "You feed the homeless."

"I ain't so sure I see it," Murph protested. "Fact is, I ain't seein' nothin' too good at the moment. I'm feelin' kind of strange and disconnected right now."

Sam Who-Am put an arm around Murph. "It's all right, Murph. I'm sorry. I got going in circles like a one-winged angel. I'm sorry. Don't be afraid."

"Why's ever'body lookin' at us so funny?" Murph mumbled, weakly pointing at the half-dozen or so people standing in a semi-circle squinting at them.

"They aren't looking at us funny, Murph. It's just the light," Sam Who-Am assured him.

"Ain't no light in here," Murph insisted. "What's happenin'?"

"Just don't be afraid," Sam Who-Am repeated, cuddling Murph tenderly. "Don't be afraid."

"Tell the truth, I always been afraid," Murph whispered. "I acted tough and tried ta hide it, but I always been afraid. Of dyin', I guess. Dyin's the worst kind of not belongin'. And now here I am, an old man. A scared old man. Whatta ya gonna do?"

Sam Who-Am rocked Murph slightly. "Oh, Murph, you always tried so hard. But you never let anyone help you. You never trusted your longing to belong. Murph, if you'd tell people you are afraid, you'd help them with their fear. Tell them, Murph. Let them be with you."

Murph looked up at the scraggly, familiar faces. As loudly as he could, he whispered to them, "Ya been standin' there listenin' like CIA wire tappers, so ya musta heard what I just told Sam Who-Am here. About my bein' scared. So whatta ya gonna do?"

Without a word, the whole group got on the floor around Murph and put their arms around whatever part of him they could. Some were crying. Then one ventured to say, "God, if you can hear this, we want ta thank you for Murph. He's sort of like Jesus to us. So take care of him now he's so sick."

And another added, "Yeah, we gotta eat." Everyone laughed a little.

Then another began to sing the only religious song she knew, which was "Onward Christian Soldiers," and others joined in for a phrase or two until no one could remember the words.

Finally, someone said, "Maybe a little wine would bring 'im around." As one, they got to their feet hopefully and went after the bottle and a glass.

Sam Who-Am whispered in Murph's ear, "Do you understand any better about connections now?"

Tears began running down Murph's cheeks again. "I don't know. Maybe. I guess I feel a little less scared myself right now," he whispered back.

Sam Who-Am smiled. "Murph, the question was never about God forgiving and loving you. It's that you could never forgive yourself or love yourself. All that endless confessing was sad. And all that homeless feeling. All that work for so little. But listen now, Murph. I'm here because there isn't much time, but don't forget it's after Easter now."

"I ain't forgettin'" Murph replied, hoarsely, "but I ain't sure what that's got ta do with anything."

"It's got to do with you, Murph," Sam Who-Am whispered excitedly. "And everybody. Easter's about a different way of seeing things. It's about connections nothing can break. Connections with God. Do you want to go and check that out with me?"

"You mean leave here? With you?" Murph asked.

"Yes," Sam Who-Am nodded.

"Where?" Murph pressed.

"Hard to explain," Sam Who-Am replied. "Different but . . . not too different from here."

Murph considered the offer for a moment. Then he asked, "How long I got ta decide?"

Sam Who-Am's lips puckered for an instant. "Until Sister Mary Martha finishes her prayers for you."

Murph nodded. "I can't believe that I believe you're an angel. But whatta ya gonna do? Listen, ya married?"

Sam Who-Am looked quizzically at him. "Married? No. Why are you asking?"

Murph smiled, "Well, if I'm goin' ta go off with ya like this, I gotta check out somethin' like that. Don't want no trouble."

"Murph!" Sam Who-Am scolded.

Murph was undaunted. "I warn ya, Sam, it's gonna be a real disappointment if ya turn out ta be one of them circus freaks."

Sam Who-Am winked. "You'd be surprised at how many varieties of angels there are, Murph. Any time people discover a connection in life, some kind of Sam Who-Am is there."

The others straggled back with a bottle of wine and a glass. They poured the wine and the glass was passed around, beginning with Murph, who seem revived for a few minutes. During that time, he wrote a simple will on a piece of a lid torn from one of the cases of empty beer bottles, and everyone present managed to scrawl their name on it as a witness.

Murph left half of his tavern to Saint Madeleine's for the purpose of feeding the homeless. The other half he left to the homeless themselves. Murph's last words were, "Maybe this'll help get two worlds together."

The words had barely passed his lips when Sister Mary Martha said, "Amen," and toppled off her prie-dieu in the convent chapel of Saint Madeleine's, dead from a massive cerebral hemorrhage but with a beatific smile on her face.

It was the same sort of smile that the rescue squad found on the face of Murph when they responded to an emergency call from his tavern. Sam Who-Am had left by then, and only among themselves did the homeless speak of the one some referred to as she, others as he, but all with awe in their voices.

Though Murph's will quickly became public information, whether it holds up in court still remains to be seen. Right now, no one is contesting it. At least not openly. Meanwhile, the only changes in Murph's Tavern are few but important. A member of Saint Madeleine's helps run the tavern jointly with a homeless person on a rotating basis, and the parish has cleaned it up a bit. Nuns and priests and church members mingle with the homeless while serving lunch, which the two groups often end up eating together.

Channel 6 has revisited to inform its viewers of this unusual circumstance. The question is whether the cameras, in panning the inside of the tavern, showed close-up the last, smallest, and perhaps most significant change in Murph's Tavern: three kodachrome pictures stuck side-by-side amidst the other mementos.

One picture shows Murph passing out soup and sandwiches to the homeless.

A second, which no one has any idea how it was taken, shows Murph smiling, sitting on the floor with a non-descript looking bag lady, surrounded by a motley but happy looking group of vagrants, all of them actually looking a little like clowns at a party.

The third shows Murph's grave, a few daffodils stuck jauntily in a beer bottle leaning against a new headstone that reads, "Patrick John Ezekiel Murphy" in smaller letters, a larger "Murph" under that, and across the top, in slightly larger letters, "It's after Easter. Whatta ya gonna do?"

Very deepest mystery

O God,
    at last I discern
        even in this dark glass of finitude,
    that the deeper mystery is goodness,
        not evil in all its demonic poses
            or all its grinding banalities;
    beauty, not nagging ugliness;
    truth, not falsehood followed however long.

The mystery is goodness, beauty, truth:
    not just goodness agreed-upon, rewarded,
        self-interest compromised but slightly;
    not just beauty of the admired surface,
        custom left unaltered by creativity;
    not just truth measured by the numbers,
        the unseen not included in its frame;
    though even these are mystery
        far from all necessity,
            as am I,
                or anything at all.

But Lord,
    the deeper mystery is something more:
        the sacrifice,
            the costly word,
                the disdained lure,
                    the just deed done unto the death;
        the keeping of breakable promises,
            the long walk of compassion,
                the unsafe witness,
                    the cross,
                       the music;
    humanity past depravity,
        all life, my life, this prayer,
            this wink of dust
                this blink of eye that sees
                    traces of forever.

Come close, now, old holy friend past full knowing,
    that I may know that this deeper mystery
        I am in, and that's in me,
           is because you have made me holy, too,
               and all this wondrous life I share;
    that this hunger, this longing
        for the goodness, beauty, truth
           that keeps breaking my heart,
              and remaking it,
               is holy
                   because all is connected,
                    all life, all worlds,
                       to you.

Come close, old holy adversary in all trusting,
    that I may trust that this urge in me
        to go on and on and on,
           is holy because you are the pull of it,
               yours the hard to hear,
               hard to resist
               summons to go on,
                   beyond defeat, discouragement, despair,
                   beyond even goodness, beauty, truth,
      to go on until I am found
           by the life I long and love and each moment live toward
               (though mostly too unknowing,
               but live toward, nonetheless,
               even through the veil of death);
           a holy life with you, and all the rest,
               in unimaginable goodness, beauty, truth,
               because it is you who, above all, beyond all,
               keeps breakable promises
                   and your grace is the very deepest
                   mystery of all.

THE ARTIST:
ED KERNS

Internationally known as an abstract painter, Ed Kerns is currently the Eugene H. Clapp Professor of Humanities and Art at Lafayette College, Easton, Pennsylvania. He holds degrees from Richmond Professional Institute (B.F.A.) and The Maryland Institute College of Art (M.F.A.), and his paintings are frequently exhibited at the Rosa Esman Gallery in New York, as well as in Paris, London, and other principal European cities. Major art magazines, including *Art News*, *Artforum*, and *Arts*, along with *The New York Times* and *The Village Voice*, have extensively reviewed his passionate, idiosyncratic style, describing his work as "imagery that communicates instantly to the viewer."

THE AUTHOR:
TED LODER

Ted Loder is the imaginative Senior Minister of the First United Methodist Church of Germantown (FUMCOG) in Philadelphia. For nearly thirty years he has encouraged and led this dynamic metropolitan congregation to the forefront of social concerns and creative artistic endeavors. FUMCOG's community involvements have included starting and supporting a medical missions program for low-income Philadelphians, a program for high-school dropouts, an off-campus urban semester for college students, and a nonprofit corporation for rehabilitating low-income housing. Other current projects provide housing in church facilities for homeless people, produce a community concert series, and promote a highly respected theater/drama group. FUMCOG is also a Public Sanctuary church and a Reconciling Congregation.

Ted Loder is a passionate, powerful preacher and lecturer widely sought throughout the United States. He received his B.D. from Yale Divinity School and an honorary doctorate from Willamette University, and has been selected by the *National Observer* as one of America's Outstanding Creative Preachers for writing and staging story and drama sermons. His published books include *GUERRILLAS OF GRACE: Prayers for the Battle*; *TRACKS IN THE STRAW: Tales Spun from the Manger*; *NO ONE BUT US: Personal Reflections on Public Sanctuary*; *EAVESDROPPING ON THE ECHOES: Voices from the Old Testament*; and, most recently, *WRESTLING THE LIGHT: Ache and Awe in the Human-Divine Struggle*.

Ted Loder is above all a visionary leader, a mystic, a prophet in his own time challenging us to re-explore traditional beliefs, re-connect with heartfelt prayer, and re-discover the whole of life.

LuraMedia Publications

BANKSON, MARJORY ZOET
Braided Streams: *Esther and a Woman's Way of Growing*
Seasons of Friendship: *Naomi and Ruth as a Pattern*

BOHLER, CAROLYN STAHL
Prayer on Wings: *A Search for Authentic Prayer*

BOZARTH, ALLA RENEE
Womanpriest: *A Personal Odyssey (Revised Edition)*

GEIGER, LURA JANE
Astonish Me, Yahweh Leader's Guide

and **PATRICIA BACKMAN**
Braided Streams Leader's Guide

and **SUSAN TOBIAS**
Seasons of Friendship Leader's Guide

and **SANDY LANDSTEDT, MARY GECKELER, PEGGIE OURY**
Astonish Me, Yahweh!: *A Bible Workbook-Journal*

JEVNE, RONNA FAY
It All Begins With Hope: *Patients, Caretakers, and the Bereaved Speak Out*

and **ALEXANDER LEVITAN**
No Time for Nonsense: *Getting Well Against the Odds*

KEIFFER, ANN
Gift of the Dark Angel: *A Woman's Journey through Depression toward Wholeness*

LODER, TED
Eavesdropping on the Echoes: *Voices from the Old Testament*
Guerrillas of Grace: *Prayers for the Battle*
No One But Us: *Personal Reflections on Public Sanctuary*
Tracks in the Straw: *Tales Spun from the Manger*
Wrestling the Light: *Ache and Awe in the Human-Divine Struggle*

LUCIANI, JOSEPH
Healing Your Habits: *Introducing Directed Imagination*

MCMAKIN, JACQUELINE
with **SONYA DYER**
Working from the Heart: *For Those Who Search for Meaning and Satisfaction in Their Work*

MEYER, RICHARD C.
One Anothering: *Biblical Building Blocks for Small Groups*

MILLETT, CRAIG
In God's Image: *Archetypes of Women in Scripture*

O'CONNOR, ELIZABETH
Search for Silence *(Revised Edition)*

SAURO, JOAN
Whole Earth Meditation: *Ecology for the Spirit*

SCHAPER, DONNA
A Book of Common Power: *Narratives Against the Current*
Stripping Down: *The Art of Spiritual Restoration*

WEEMS, RENITA J.
Just a Sister Away: *A Womanist Vision of Women's Relationships in the Bible*

LuraMedia Women's Series

BORTON, JOAN
Drawing from the Women's Well: *Reflections from the Life Passage of Menopause*

CARTLEDGE-HAYES, MARY
To Love Delilah: *Claiming the Women of the Bible*

DAHL, JUDY
River of Promise: *Two Women's Story of Love and Adoption*

DUERK, JUDITH
Circle of Stones: *Woman's Journey to Herself*

RUPP, JOYCE
The Star in My Heart: *Experiencing Sophia, Inner Wisdom*

SCHAPER, DONNA
Superwoman Turns 40: *The Story of One Woman's Intentions to Grow Up*

LuraMedia, Inc. , 7060 Miramar Rd., Suite 104, San Diego, CA 92121
Books for Healing and Hope, Balance and Justice.